Coming out of my shell

The memoirs of

Jerry the Tortoise

by

Alison Sprigg

ISBN: 978-172465-762-6

Contents

Dedication

Acknowledgements

Dedication

For all my family: past and present, human and animal.

Acknowledgements

Sincere thanks to my editor, for his invaluable expertise, advice and encouragement, and to all my family and friends for their unfailing support and belief in this project.

I'd also like to acknowledge the work of the real Hampshire Tortoise Society in promoting tortoise welfare, and to thank the real British Chelonia Group for arranging the eventual re-homing of the equally real Jerry!

Chapter 1: Cold call
By way of introduction

A fridge probably seems an unlikely place from which to introduce myself. After all, someone like me, being a tortoise of Mediterranean descent, is more usually associated in any biped's mind with warmth and sunshine.

So I should really start by reassuring you that what I enjoy most, naturally enough, is spending endless summer days languidly soaking up all those life-enhancing rays from the sun, through my individually-designed and intricately-patterned shell. In fact, my shell could reasonably be described as my very own, personalised solar panel.

But we tortoises do need to chill out, too, when nature prompts us to do so as part of the ordained rhythm of the seasons. A spell of winter *in*activity perfectly balances all that summertime activity, which consists of sunlit days spent foraging for the tastiest dandelions, strawberries and lettuce leaves, strolling around my garden and then finding just the right spot for a nap in hazily dappled sunshine...

Although the chilling-out time for us chelonians is generally called hibernation, I always think it should more accurately be called low-burnation. This is because, under that protective shell of mine, my internal functions slow down to such a degree (so to speak) that I need very little energy to keep me going through the long winter's slumber. Consequently, with a heart rate that's slowed down to one beat per minute, who needs to burn lots of calories?

Of course, chilling out for the whole winter does mean that I miss all those end-of-year festivities which seem so important to the bipeds, though I suspect that quite a few of them – notably the female of the species, in my experience – would actually be very happy to join me in my fridge, for the duration. But it strikes me that there's a growing desire, amongst the bipeds generally, to sidestep the winter season and let it take care of itself. Very understandable. Meanwhile, we in the ancient Chelonian Order of Reptiles (which consists of us tortoises and our cousins the turtles), have been doing exactly that for millennia, so we know it works. I should just mention that although the Chelonian Order might sound like some sort of secret society, built on the desire to retreat into a collective shell, it's actually not secretive at all. So I'd be very happy to dispense my very own version of seasonal hospitality, but it might be a bit tricky, as I must warn you that the space in my refrigerated winter quarters is somewhat limited. Personally, though, I'd highly recommend a long winter's nap to anyone, of any species, particularly in this cold northern climate.

Now, you might be thinking that even this cold northern climate isn't usually quite as deliberately cold as the inside of a fridge, so I'd better explain.

My name is Jerry, and I'm a Greek tortoise. We're also called spur-thigh tortoises, but I think myself that Greek is a more stylish name, as well as a more apt description. When you come to think of it, other species don't name themselves primarily for the state of their thighs, so I don't really see why we should. But at least in our case, there's a general consistency to our spurred thighs: I should think that if the bipeds tried defining themselves in that way, it might cause all sorts of problems, as the rest of us can't help noticing a certain disparity in the shape, and more alarmingly the size, of different bipeds' thighs. Perhaps, though, the term spur-thigh is meant purely as a compliment, as we Greek tortoises like to spur ourselves ever onwards, even if it does have to be rather slowly. Actually, I think my formal title should really be *Jerry the Greek Tortoise PhD (almost)*, as I once attended a psychology lecture at the University of Bangor, by special invitation of the Vice-Chancellor, no less.

That was when I was accompanying my family of bipeds on a trip to Wales, but I spent quite a few years living with them here in southern England, mostly, which is quite northerly enough for me. I would spend my summers meandering happily around the garden, supervising the growing of my own crops such as dandelions, clover and wild strawberries, selecting the most succulent morsels to eat, accepting the tasty titbits brought to me by my bipeds (cucumber, lettuce and grapes are my own particular favourites), and finding soft, comfortable places to while away sunny afternoons. But the problem with that otherwise delightful garden, was that it offered no really suitable site where I could dig myself a safe and cosy *hibernaculum*. That's the old Latin way of saying 'tent for winter quarters', by the way. I originally come from a proud line of Greek tortoises, my ancestry going right back to our patriarch Ptolemy the Greek (Tortoise), who was actually quite a famous academic in his day. Over time, then, as a

9

young tortoise and from my vantage point on the sun-soaked wall of an ancient, ruined temple, I was able to absorb at least something of a classical education, along with those timeless Mediterranean rays.

Anyway, my summer quarters in the bipeds' English country garden were perfectly charming: I had my own brick-built shelter under a red tiled roof, which was lined with straw and was extremely comfortable for balmy nights. Known as the Shell Garage, it was surrounded by its own private gardens, where I had a lawn and shrubbery, with flower beds and a selection of my favourite crops. Plus my own shallow paddling pool which, as I'm a tortoise not a turtle, provided quite sufficient water for me. I liked to use it both for drinking and for a soothing wallow, on those occasional scorching days which do happen, even in this northern climate, when I would need to cool my shell with a little gentle splashing. I would then go and settle down in the dim, cool interior of my Shell Garage, since even my purpose-built, integral solar panel has sometimes had enough sun. I've always felt rather sorry for the bipeds, who apparently need to protect their skin from the sun's natural rays, by rubbing a special cream onto themselves.

But the Shell Garage simply couldn't provide enough protection for me during the winter months. This evidently worried my bipeds when I first arrived to live with them in Hampshire. It had been a busy time for me, as I'd been living by myself for quite a long while, in Cornwall, and then I'd had a nasty accident that autumn involving a stream, just before I met the biped family and went to live with them. I was very glad to be helped out of that cold, muddy water, and then I was finally able to go to the vet for an operation. An animal had trodden on me when I was living by myself; I hadn't seen it coming, as I'm partially blind, but it had damaged part of my shell and one of my front legs. My leg had to be bandaged for some time after the operation, but I didn't mind that at all, because it didn't hurt any more, and the dietary supplement which the vet gave me, to take with my meals, was helping my shell to get stronger, too.

The result of all this interruption to my routine was that my hibernation was delayed that year, which meant I was still awake at the bipeds' festive season. They brought a small fir tree into the house, hung bits of coloured glass on it, and put it on a stand beside the big French windows. And that's what caused the trouble, really. You see, I liked to go and stand beside the big French windows, too, so that I could feel closer to the wintry garden while my system was still slowing down towards hibernation.

One day – it was actually the day of the winter solstice and I was finally beginning to feel a little drowsy – I noticed a shaft of gentle winter sunshine falling on the soft, comfy carpet, but on the other side of the fir tree. We tortoises prefer to move in a straight line, going over, under or straight through an obstacle rather than around it, so that's what I did. It's all a matter of instinct, you see. So I suppose my thighs did indeed spur me onwards. It took me quite a while to get through the fir tree, or rather, through its slightly precarious stand, but I still had plenty of strength left, after the good autumn snacks I'd been eating outside the Shell Garage, plus the vet's medicine; anyway, I needed the exercise before settling down to my delayed sleep. Luckily the stand was only made of lightweight plastic, arranged as two cross-pieces forming four legs with four equal triangles between them.

As you can no doubt tell, that's my classical education, again, which comes in very handy on occasions like this: I found that any one of the triangles would be just the right size for my shell – a right-angled triangle, as it were. So all I had to do was simply to keep on pushing, making full use of my now well-conditioned shell, until eventually the stand gave way and I could make my slow, deliberate way through. The fir tree made quite an impressive noise as it fell, stand and all, but fortunately for me, neither the tree itself, nor any of its glass bits, hit me on the way down. And happily that shaft of sunshine was still there, on the other side of the wreckage.

My bipeds were very nice about the little accident to their fir tree, and said it didn't matter in the least, as long as I was unhurt. But I was pleased to find that once they'd picked the tree up, re-attached all its coloured glass, and repaired its sadly mangled stand, they stood it at the opposite end of the room from the big French windows.

By the time my second winter with the bipeds came round, they'd worked out the best way to ensure that I could have a peaceful winter's sleep. I was rather touched that they'd done a lot of research on my behalf, into the theory and practice of hibernation: in fact, bipeds seem very keen to study this aspect of the chelonian lifestyle, though I doubt whether they could put it into practice for themselves. Anyway, the latest hibernation technique is, I believe, known as Relaxed Reptile Refrigeration, which just goes to prove that a good grounding in the Three Rs is essential to the intellectual and emotional well-being of any self-respecting tortoise.

Turning to the practicalities of hibernation, though, and the main requirements for a *hibernaculum* are that it should be safe, secure and ideally kept at a constant temperature. It needs to be cool enough to keep my heart going at that steady rate of one beat per minute; not so cold that my heart could stop completely, of course, but not so warm that I could wake up when I'm supposed to be still asleep. This is why bipeds in general have had to be discouraged from their notion of trying to help us tortoises to a comfortable hibernation by making us snug in straw-lined cardboard boxes, which they would then put in a garden shed for the winter. During a mild spell of weather, the tortoise could wake up and simply suffocate inside the box. Ugh. (We reptiles don't shiver, but a nasty crawling feeling has just crept all over my shell.)

But once I've quite naturally stopped eating during the autumn, and processed the food still in my system to make the best use of it during the winter, my metabolism slows right down to its minimum level. Then I can sleep peacefully, until nature nudges me into wakefulness once more, to see what the resurgent spring has to offer to an equally resurgent reptile.

The bipeds' research apparently showed that the optimum temperature for my winter comfort is 6°C, so they decided that the best place to keep a constant and controlled temperature for hibernation would be inside a fridge. Obviously it's not the sort of *hibernaculum* I would have chosen for myself, but I must say it's remarkably effective, and surprisingly comfortable. And really, I have to admit that all that autumnal digging under a carefully-selected shrub was very hard work. Tedious, too, as of course I dig very slowly, and the amount of earthwork needed, courtesy of my admittedly short legs, to make a cosy resting-place large enough for my entire shell, was disproportionately large (as Ptolemy Tortoise would no doubt have described it).

Given all the circumstances, then, I was perfectly happy to accept my bipeds' suggestion of winter quarters in a fridge for that second winter in Hampshire, and it provided me with such a successful and peaceful hibernation, that I've subscribed to the principles of the Three Rs ever since. Needless to say, I've always had my own private fridge, completely separate from the one used by the bipeds for storing their food. After all, it would be very alarming to find myself being mistaken for a Cornish pasty, if I'd taken lodgings in the family-sized version.

But, as I mentioned just now, my own fridge is a surprisingly comfortable place to while away the winter. When I'm just about to fall into my deep, heart-slowing sleep, my various bipeds have always helped me to snuggle down in my straw-lined box and, in a gesture which I found rather touching, my Hampshire family would then cover my shell with an old tea-towel, by way of my very own duvet. In case I should care to browse while I drowse, this features pictures of Cornish gardens, as a gentle reminder of the years I'd already spent living in Cornwall, and where I first met this particular family. In fact, I still use my *Cornish gardens* duvet nowadays. Then my bipeds lightly fold down the lid of my bed-box, leaving it open just enough for the air to circulate. It all provides a neat four-poster effect, with the shelves of the fridge being draped in sundry salads and fruits, which tends to happen when bipeds need to store extra food in my fridge, 'specially for their end-of-year festive season.

Alongside me, once I'm snugly tucked away in my bed-box, my fridge contains a glass of water. This isn't in case I should get thirsty, as of course I don't need to get up for a drink, once I've fallen asleep, but it has a thermometer and a humidity monitor in it, connected by wires through the door seal to a digital read-out panel. If the temperature or humidity varies too much inside my fridge, bedlam ensues on the control panel, apparently, with alarms and flashing lights. It's like having one of those panic buttons, to summon help if required; I can rest assured, as it were, that if the conditions in my fridge should change, my bipeds would know immediately and could make the necessary adjustments for me.

Even though this means that I have my own personalised version of a panic button, the bipeds have always checked on me regularly, to make sure I'm not losing too much weight during hibernation. I do lose a little, naturally, particularly when it's nearly time to wake up. So I have my own digital scale which has a flat plastic weighing platform, so that the bipeds can weigh me without waking me: the slight movement of being gently lifted out of my box, put on the scale and then returned to my straw and my duvet, isn't enough to disturb my slumbers.

This high-tech approach by the bipeds is all very well, as far as it goes, but of course there is one potential problem with the Three Rs. Fridges run on electricity, and sometimes, so I understand, the bipeds have trouble with the electricity supply to their houses. It seems that bipeds in this country are particularly prone to this problem during harsh winter weather, which is exactly when I'd have thought they would be most in need of their electricity. Anyway, my own bipeds came up with an effective solution for me: a totally separate electricity generator, just for my *hibernaculum*, so that if the household's supply should ever fail, my fridge would keep going. As a gesture of thanks for such thoughtfulness, I felt the least I could do would be to allow my bipeds to store their extra food in my fridge each December.

And so I could sleep the cold months peacefully away, surrounded by all that salad and fruit to scent my midwinter dreams, naturally enough, with the promise of spring...

Chapter 2: Gardeners' Questing Time
When the grass really is greener

With the bipeds' well-intentioned habit of checking on me regularly throughout the winter, I've always been guaranteed a supply of good fresh air in my refrigerated bed-box. So, when the gentlest hint of spring starts to permeate the atmosphere and to make its way even as far as my fridge, I sense the first faint calling of the new season. It's a call that no earth-bound creature can resist, as insistent as the growth of the new vegetation to which I start feeling the instinctive longing to return, whether from a dugout in the ground or a box in the fridge. Meanwhile, the scent of fresh salads continues to waft over me in my fridge from time to time, as a promise of the pleasant, balmy days to come.

Gradually, then, I start to stir underneath my *Cornish gardens* duvet, shaking off sleep along with my coverings. Then I realise it's time to leave my cosy *hibernaculum* and venture out into the world once more. Well, not quite out into the world straight away, since my first stop, nowadays, is the *vivarium* set up for me by my bipeds. This is my own private living area inside the bipeds' house. It's very useful for when I first get up from hibernation and for when the weather is too unpleasant, in early spring, for me to shelter comfortably in the Shell Garage. To be quite honest, I'm not really too keen on my *vivarium*, as I find it horribly restricting to walk around the same, rather uninteresting, area all the time. But I'd never want to let my bipeds know that, after all the

17

trouble they took in setting it up for me, so I walk around it anyway, and try to look interested.

The *vivarium*, which is made of wood, is actually quite large – it takes up about the same amount of space as a biped family's sofa – and it's lined with a mixture of straw and shredded paper. I suspect that the paper element of the mix consists of shredded bills which the bipeds would rather not think about, although they like to say that they need to add paper simply because, by the time spring comes, there's not much usable straw available. It's a perfectly comfortable mix to walk and lie on; just rather boring, with no interesting smells or textures. Fixed to one side of the *vivarium* is a sort of scaffold arrangement supporting an overhead gantry, to which the bipeds attach my heat and sun lamps. The overall effect is rather like one of those gantries you see at fixed intervals on motorways, with flashing signs, except of course that I don't ever feel a desire to dash round my *vivarium* at high speed, or to have my heat and sun lamps flashing. And my *vivarium* has no queues.

But my first need on waking up is, quite naturally, a bath – well, wouldn't anyone, after spending four months in bed? In my case, though, it's mainly for rehydration, as I can absorb water through the surface of my shell, but it's very refreshing to stretch my neck and duck my head briefly under the warm water, while I'm at it. On the subject of ducks, I don't go in for any of the bath-time accoutrements so beloved of the bipeds: no plastic duck, far less any bubble bath, shower cap or back-brush for me. Just a gentle soak in my personal bathtub, which is a large, oblong plastic container with reassuringly high and rigid sides, as I like to wade around its edges once I've finished wallowing in the warm, shallow water. Just to get the measure of it.

Then it's out of the bath to be enveloped in a welcomingly soft towel, where I can be gently patted dry by my bath attendant (one of my obliging bipeds), all of which probably makes me sound more like an ancient Roman than a Greek. Just like a biped, I do like to make sure that all my important little places are thoroughly dried: I'm particularly fussy about those places which join my shell, along with my face and neck, and my legs and claws. Unlike a biped, though, I don't need to use any type of moisturiser on my scaly but self-sufficient reptilian skin; not even any Shell Oil-type lubricant.

The next stage in my springtime resurgence is a few sessions under my heat and sun lamps, back in my *vivarium*. It's important for me get the angle of my shell exactly right, in order to take full advantage of the up-to-date facilities offered by this biped-run chelonian health and fitness centre. I would find a deckchair somewhat uncomfortable, of course, so I settle for plumping up the shredded credit card bills, along with the straw, nudging it all into place until my shell is comfortably propped up at just the right angle to make best use of the UV rays and the gentle heat coming from my lamps.

Then I can settle down and bask contentedly, being perfectly happy to sunbathe without the biped-style sunglasses or glossy magazine. I don't really go in for much in the way of pampering, either, in my private spa, as a full day's treatment session would be a little too much of a good thing. Most years, I find that I don't even need to get my claws done.

Then, after all that preparation and a celebratory snack of cucumber and watercress in my *vivarium*, it's off to the garden, my biped-manufactured outdoor habitat. The garden is one of the benefits of domestication, being perfectly suited for life in this northern climate. The smell of the fresh grass is strong and sweet, tickling my nostrils and enticing me to stretch my legs out fully as I wander with renewed pleasure around the garden, sniffing out the promise of all the seasonal delights to come. The lawn is already dotted with newly emerging dandelions, although strangely, the bipeds don't seem to be as fond of finding dandelions on the lawn as I am. From my vantage point close to the rapidly warming earth, I feel new life springing up once again, out of the drab stillness which was a northern winter. But being a true creature of the earth, I'm completely at one with the new growth all around me, whether northern or southern, cultivated or wild.

Best of all, though, is the sheer joy of feeling the natural rays of the sun on my shell. It's my very own rechargeable battery: my energy levels rise until, feeling irresistibly fully-charged, I charge around the lawn for the pure pleasure of being alive and making use of all that stored energy. Then it's off to my favourite sunny spot beneath the hyacinths and the budding daffodils, where my shell is sheltered and where my bipeds like to come and seek me out at lunchtime, bringing me early salad leaves, with tomato and grated carrot, followed by a few carefully-skinned grapes for dessert.

Meanwhile, the bipeds like to perform their own rather quaint rite of welcoming the spring, which involves placing a few large, brightly-wrapped chocolate eggs in various hiding-places around the garden. This part of the ritual is performed by the adults of the species; the juveniles then come out into the garden carrying baskets decorated with colourful tissue paper, and search for the eggs which they discover and place joyfully in the baskets, to the accompaniment of delighted shrieks. This rite is known as an Easter Egg Hunt, the origins of which go back many years. I find it all rather touching, particularly as it stirs within me a half-forgotten memory of my own hatchling days, and an even vaguer recollection of an egg, long ago, with its shell cracking open...

My only involvement in my biped companions' version, though, has always been to lend them a favourite hiding-place for their eggs. So, for that one day each year, the Shell Garage becomes the Eggshell Garage. Perhaps it's a shame that I don't eat chocolate, or feel any inclination to take part in the Easter Egg Hunt, otherwise I could at least join my bipeds for a celebratory chocolate tort(e).

Despite the bipeds' bringing tasty titbits to the garden for me, I do enjoy foraging for myself, naturally; just like the juvenile bipeds during their Easter Egg Hunt. This instinct is strong in me, right from the first day of my springtime return to the garden. In fact, on seeing me making my steady way in amongst the springtime blooms in the borders, my Hampshire bipeds would cheerfully announce:

"Stand by your (flower)beds; His Slowliness is back!"

They seemed to find that amusing. Actually it's a totally inaccurate description, as I am by no means always a slow mover: although I'm sure it would be extremely uncomfortable for me to break into an outright run, I can achieve a variety of paces, from gentle ambling to purposeful power-walking. Running would hold no attraction for me, in any case, having witnessed its after-effects on various bipeds. Their faces tend to become unusually colourful, turning a variety of interesting shades from pinkish red through to darkest purple, while they pant just as noisily as any dog, and perspire more than any other creature I've ever come across. All this visible manifestation of sheer over-exertion tends to be accompanied by a triumphant recital of the amount, and speed, of the frenetic activity which brought on so much proudly displayed discomfort. Personally, I prefer to circumnavigate my summertime world like a slow but determined jogger, though without the earphones or the bottle of water usually sported by exercise-conscious bipeds.

My Hampshire biped family didn't tend to run madly around the garden itself, although using their rather unpleasantly noisy and smelly petrol-driven mower seemed to have much the same effects. This machine appeared to have a mind of its own. Once it had been successfully started, which usually took a considerable amount of effort by the increasingly red-faced male biped, it would shake and splutter as it roared into life, as if desperate to be off on its mission of destruction.

The most dramatic scenes would occur on those occasions when this contraption's throttle got stuck. Something to do with its enhanced gearing, so I understand. But whatever the reason, it became a truly awesome sight. At the first sign of the mower's starting to speed up, the male biped would cling on grimly, waggling the lever on the handle and starting to trot, simply to keep up with it. Suddenly the machine's speed seemed to increase alarmingly, causing it to career around the lawn in a cloud of evil-smelling smoke, roaring madly and dragging the unfortunate biped in its wake. By this time he would be running hard, still waggling the lever desperately. Meanwhile, the female biped had usually emerged from the house by now; she would jump up and down and yell, trying to make herself heard above the mower's roar:

"Mind Jerry!"

This seemed to concentrate the mind of the male biped very successfully, and he would pull himself together, insofar as that was possible in the circumstances. But by that stage I'd already retreated to the safety of a distant flower bed, or to the Shell Garage, from where I would watch the exhausted biped eventually bringing the mechanical monster under control, before it could achieve its apparent aim of destroying the entire garden. Although I made sure I was never near enough for it to strike me, it strikes me that lawn-mowing is really not the favourite activity of any biped.

Bipeds generally seem to enjoy digging in the garden, though, and planting various crops, which I quite naturally appreciate. I do my best to encourage my own bipeds, particularly in the summertime, when a bout of digging can have the same alarming effects on a biped as a bout of running (or lawn-mowing). They also put a lot of effort into watering my crops, so one summer I decided that the time had come to show my appreciation by helping them out a bit, with a rather more scientific approach to the subject of irrigation.

The Hampshire garden contained two large, interconnected fishponds raised at different heights above the level of the earth and surrounded by brickwork, presumably designed with the very considerate intention of ensuring I couldn't fall in. The lower pond had a small fountain powered by an underground pump. The water circulated from the upper to the lower pond, where it cascaded elegantly from the fountain before returning to the pump, via a pipe running across a slight slope – below which were my most productive pastures. All that lovely water, two reservoirs' worth, simply going round and round in a loop. So I thought very hard, while basking in the sweet, sunny grass during the first warm spell of summer, and I came up with an idea for an irrigation system to keep my crops watered if we should have a drought.

You see, I'd realised that instead of unrolling the big hosepipe every summer evening, my bipeds could make far more constructive use of their existing but woefully under-utilised facilities. That's called lateral thinking, I believe. (Ptolemy's influence, again.)

The idea came to me when I noticed that there was a slight fissure in the fishpond, though not on a large scale (or indeed on any scale, the ponds being devoid

24

of fish and their scales in any case). Nevertheless, that fissure was enough to cause a noticeable leakage from the lower pond directly into my pasture. How to enlarge on that drought-beating potential initially seemed imponderable, so to speak, but the more I pondered, the more crystal-clear the solution became.

I decided I ought to test my idea first, before there could be any hint of a drought, and it worked. In fact, it worked even better than I'd expected. I emptied the ponds. Both of them, completely, which was something of a surprise; perhaps even more so to my bipeds than to me.

Having carefully drawn up my plans, I started by excavating underneath the pipe on the slope above my pastures, working my way steadily towards the pump. Just to see how everything was connected. As I dug deeper, prospecting happily, the top of my shell was constantly rubbing away at the connection between two sections of the pipe, and gradually loosening it…

So I ended up by unplugging the entire system. I must admit that the onset of the flood was rather sudden, so at that point I abandoned my dig as hastily as I could. But the lower reservoir emptied surprisingly quickly, which meant that my shell was irrigated, as well as my crops. It was worth it, though, for peace of mind: I now knew that I could circumvent any future hosepipe ban, and ensure that my crops would always be well-watered to retain their succulence.

Once I'd dried off in the sunshine and returned to the scene of the grime, I was very pleased to see that my bipeds – after they'd recovered from their surprise at my feat of engineering – had courteously re-attached the pipe and re-filled both the reservoirs, in case I should find it necessary to turn on my independent irrigation system once again. In fact, the whole system became known in the family, scientifically, as the Jerry Can.

Another aspect of scientific discovery which bipeds generally have adopted, apparently from the example set by us chelonians, is the use of solar energy. Sunshine is, of course, woefully scarce in this northern clime, so I felt very reassured, on emerging into the garden one spring, to see the steps which my own bipeds had taken to make the best use of what little sunshine there is. Glancing up at their house, I was pleased to see that its roof seemed to have been transformed into a sort of glazed shell, with glossy plates evidently designed to absorb the sun's rays in much the same way as the scutes, or plates, on my own shell are designed to do. Very sensible. But judging by the ladders which were strewn about the place, and the continued presence of the workmen, it appeared that these artificial plates cause far more trouble to a biped, than natural ones cause to a tortoise.

Then there was the summer when my bipeds decided to have the windows and doors of their house replaced. Again, very sensible, but it did involve a great deal of activity, both indoors and out, with bipeds hammering, shouting, leaving ladders all over the place and parking enormous windows on the lawn. Each day, before the workmen appeared in the garden, I would make sure I was pre-parked at the entrance to the Shell Garage, ready to fend off anyone who might become over-enthusiastic and start trying to glaze it, or to fit modern inconveniences like doors. Still, the workmen eventually saw their way clear, as it were, to finishing the job, which was a relief to all concerned. After all, no glazier likes to have a stained glass reputation.

With so much frenetic activity going on in the garden each summer, I would often wonder whether it was entirely safe to leave my bipeds in charge all winter, while I was peacefully asleep in my fridge. But as each summer drew to its close, I resigned myself to trusting them once again, and turned my mind to reflecting on how well my own crops had done, regardless of weather or interruptions. My dandelion crop invariably did very well, my strawberries were suitably small and sweet, and there in my Hampshire garden, I always enjoyed a variety of delicious flowers such as wild geranium, speedwell (though by the end of summer I personally don't speed well) and, perhaps appropriately, forget-me-not.

Autumn always brought its own pleasures, too: late shafts of warm sunshine, the last tasty clover leaves, extra bedding in my Shell Garage and a refrigerated hibernation to look forward to, courtesy of my faithful family of bipeds.

But I haven't always lived in domesticated comfort and a protected environment: far from it.

Chapter 3: The tortoise and the heir
A Greek Odyssey

The Isles of Greece contain many ancient memories and fabled creatures. Strictly speaking, I'm not really one of them, as I was actually hatched in Morocco. I am most definitely a Greek tortoise, though, a true *testudo graeca* and heir to my ancestors' successful colonization of various territories over the years. It was a slow and sometimes tortuous process, naturally enough, but all achieved without any of the general upheaval associated with the bipeds' territorial campaigns.

Greek tortoises have lived for aeons not only in Greece itself, but in a wide area stretching from Africa to southern Europe, eventually migrating to northern Europe and, ultimately, even as far as Britain. Of course, travelling tortoises have often made use of biped help, particularly in such matters as sea-crossings, and also land journeys over terrain which might otherwise be tricky for a reptile. But throughout history, the bipeds in general have proved themselves to be perfectly amenable, even to the extent of assuming that our collaboration has been purely for their own benefit.

Just as an example: in former and more barbaric times the sea-faring variety of bipeds, before setting sail aboard their pirate ships or whaling vessels, used to invade chelonian colonies and collect tortoises to put into their ship's hold – as ballast. But any tortoise worth his sea-salt could live in a ship's hold for over a year without food or water. So even if the voyage was long, the physical conditions presented no major problem, or at least they could be tolerated. On docking in their next port, the sailors would unload their 'ballast', either exchanging tortoises for things they needed, with the local bipeds, or simply leaving their now unwanted chelonian cargo to its own devices – which, owing to the adaptability of our species, were usually successful. And so new tortoise colonies were established.

Meanwhile, back in North Africa, the Moroccan bipeds had developed a habit of keeping Greek tortoises in the souks of cities such as Marrakech, to sell as pets. The compensation for those particular tortoises, having survived the bipeds' noisy marketplace, was to arrive at rather more suitable accommodation, usually in another country. That practice went on for many generations, but it's now well on the way to being stamped out completely: the biped authorities have put their collective foot down with a firm hand, so to speak.

All this biped-assisted migration has meant that our species is now thoroughly widespread in the world, and capable of living in widely differing climates, too. This has proved to be a very fortunate characteristic in my own case, since over the years I've become something of a well-travelled tortoise of the world.

I don't keep count of years in the same way as bipeds do – I'm ageless, preferring simply to concern myself with the rhythm of the changing seasons. My hatchling days, though, were undoubtedly many years ago. I spent my earliest times very happily, in a peaceful colony on the coastal steppes of Morocco. We tortoises roamed freely amongst the lush vegetation, co-existing contentedly with a wide range of other creatures including various lizards, frogs and birds, all of us undisturbed by any biped activity.

But our peaceful way of life was shattered when the world of the bipeds went to war with itself. Terrible noises reached us, while the earth was ripped by explosions and the sky was lit by fire: the bipeds were fighting each other for possession of the whole of North Africa. One faction apparently called its campaign *Operation Torch*, which certainly seemed to be an apt description of the hellfire being aimed by both biped factions at each other, while the rest of us were being caught in the crossfire. Towering machines arrived, each one rolling along on crushing runners and with a long arm sticking out in front. Occasionally a biped's head would pop up, to peer out from the top of one of these machines; and so the biped inside his offensive weapon became a travesty of the tortoise inside his defensive shell. But this was, in fact, simply a modern version of the ancient bipeds' attempt at tortoise-style protection, which they achieved by linking their shields together to form a shell. Those ancient bipeds, having learned by imitation, even named their protection system after us tortoises: they called it '*testudo* formation'. Its Latin name wasn't *t. graeca*, which refers solely to our genus; it must have been *t. romana*.

Anyway, these modern versions of *t. romana* were followed by ranks of identical-looking bipeds, marching past on their way to the coast. All this upheaval was leading to a general migration of bipeds and animals alike. I decided to join the exodus: what with the destruction and the general confusion, emigration now seemed the best option. Instinctively, my aim was to travel to Greece, my spiritual homeland. But I would need to hitch a lift with the bipeds, to get to the coast in the first place, and to cross the sea in the second place.

I waited until a contingent of bipeds paused nearby to rest overnight. It was easy enough to climb in unnoticed amongst their luggage, and settle down to be driven to the port, ready to embark on my very own voyage of discovery. My quarters were adequate, though not exactly luxurious: I'd stowed myself away in a small crate of metal egg-shapes, each one covered in plates which resembled the scutes on the shell of a rather small tortoise, but with a sort of pin at one end. It seemed as good a place as any to settle down, so I withdrew tightly into my shell and tried to look like one of the metal imitation tortoises. Actually, once on board ship I was perfectly content to be travelling in my own private cabin, having no particular desire to roam around the ship's hold as a piece of ballast: much better to travel cabin-class than steerage. So, when selecting my travelling-box, I'd carefully chosen a small, insignificant-looking crate which probably wouldn't be wanted on the voyage. There was a notice on the outside of my cabin, though it meant nothing to me, of course: *Grenades*.

Whatever use grenades might be to a biped, I can't say that travelling amongst a lot of hard, metal egg-shapes was particularly comfortable for a tortoise. But at least their pins didn't start falling out all over the place, and they did underpin me fairly well against the motion of the vessel. Nobody bothered me; in fact, nobody came near me throughout my time on board, so I slept the voyage away as peacefully as I could, in my metal-cushioned berth, and waited to disembark. It wasn't a long voyage, in any case, and the sea was mercifully calm. When the ship docked at a port on one of the Greek islands, I found more biped-induced chaos; their factions had evidently been fighting here, too, with the inevitable destructive consequences for everything and everyone around them. Which is ironic, really, when you consider that the bipeds like to refer to Greece as their Cradle of Western Civilization.

Amidst the chaos and noise of their own concerns, none of the bipeds noticed one small and actually very well-camouflaged tortoise, disembarking from his crate on the quayside and then making his own way unobtrusively in the opposite direction from the soldiering bipeds. They were setting off to march along the coastal road, and since they clearly had no interest in the wooded hill rising towards the interior of the island, that direction seemed the obvious route for me to take.

Making my slow and steady way inland, I skirted the edge of a biped village which lay nestled amongst shady pine trees. So that strong instinct of mine, to continue in a straight line regardless of obstacles, was tempered on this occasion by the equally strong instinct of self-preservation. This was because I soon found out that these were real pine trees, immense and well-rooted, not the small indoor version which, many years later, I would send crashing to the floor in an English house. Happily for me, though, these Greek houses were situated in temptingly lush gardens, shaded by cypress and fruit trees. I would sleep under a convenient bush at night, and emerge once the first rays of Mediterranean sunshine had roused me. To stoke up my system for the day, I was able to take full advantage of the succulent salad leaves and flower heads on offer, since the bipeds had so thoughtfully planted them within easy foraging distance of a wayfaring tortoise.

Having breakfasted long before any of the indigenous bipeds became active in their gardens, I would set off again, feeling refreshed by sleep, sunshine and food. I forged a steady path away from the village and its olive groves, always concealed by roadside vegetation and always seeking the sanctuary of the hillside just ahead of me, which at that time was completely uninhabited by warring bipeds.

Eventually I left the village behind me, with the sea beyond it and the hill rising ahead. In those days I had very good eyesight, and as I slowly swung my head from side to side – as we tortoises like to do – I could take in the entire panoramic view of the glittering sea and the welcoming hills. Now I felt I could relax. Emerging from a bush to stretch out luxuriously in the sunshine and feel the first warmth of the day, I could breakfast at my leisure on the patches of dandelion and clover spread out in the shade of the trees, before exploring my new surroundings at a suitably slow pace. As I made my way even further from the biped village, familiar noises and smells became stronger, until I found myself in the vicinity of my own kind once again.

The mating season was over for that year by the time I arrived, so I didn't need to get involved in any fights with the local males. That was fortunate, really, since my long journey had cost me a great deal of energy, despite the unintentional help of the bipeds with their ship and their gardens. I was probably too exhausted even to mate (which can be a lengthy process for us tortoises, since we're slow and steady in all things), let alone to fight for the right to mate. But it had been worth every step, every discomfort and every danger, to arrive at the place on which I'd set my sights, the natural haven for us Greek tortoises: our very own World Heritage Site. For the rest of that long, languid summer, I set about immersing myself in my new surroundings, and in the classic traditions of our Greek culture, handed down from Ptolemy Tortoise to generations of his heirs, on the slopes of our native hills.

In fact, my ancestors must long ago have shared this particular hill with the bipeds. Perhaps, like Greek tortoises, those Greek bipeds were able to establish their niche in whatever environment they found themselves. And the particular niche which those ancient bipeds had established in their hilltop environment seemed to have been one of their renowned temples. Lying in ruins now, its shallow steps and low walls made ideal sun-drenched basking sites for any number of tortoises. Plenty of fresh, juicy vegetation was there for the nibbling, too, growing amongst cracks in the stone and in succulent patches in the shade of the surrounding bushes.

In this idyllic spot I happily absorbed knowledge along with sunshine, amidst the ruins of that ancient civilization where physical and intellectual wellbeing were inextricably linked, and where nature and culture could co-exist in harmony. Naturally, Greek tortoises don't go in for Greek biped-style Olympic Games, although those original, ancient Games did actually include mental exercises as well as physical ones, along with cultural activities and music. As far as music is concerned, we tortoises only sing when we're mating, and even then it's entirely the preserve of the male of our species, with only solo performances taking place. No harmonising or romantic duets for us, and of course the only Beatles we come across are the type which make their way among crevices or along the ground. So our music is neither classical nor popular, in biped terms – although a colony of tortoises in the mating season could perhaps be described as a male voice choir – but to us it's an instinctive and integral part of the rhythm of life itself: soul music, in fact.

That leaves the Olympic mental exercises and cultural activities. Certainly the emphasis on balance, proportion and symmetry is every bit as crucial to modern Greek tortoises as it was to ancient Greek bipeds: particularly when we're forging a precarious path along a ruined temple wall, to find a lofty basking place from which to contemplate the equally lofty ideals of our existence.

Those ideals include, naturally enough, the annual ritual of mating. Every male tortoise likes to get into tip-top condition in the spring, once he's woken from hibernation and eaten a few good meals. Fighting fit, in fact, since in any tortoise colony, a fight with at least one other male is the usual prerequisite to consorting with one's chosen female. But by the time my first mating season in Greece came around, I felt ready for any such Herculean-style feat. Having dug my winter *hibernaculum* under a bush, I scraped my way out again in the spring, heaving the clods of earth aside and then making my way – a little unsteadily, perhaps – towards the nearest clover patch. This was all a very different process from my later awakenings with my biped family and their fridge. All over that Greek tortoise colony, small landslides seemed to be going on as, one by one, each tortoise roused, hoisted himself (or herself, of course) from the earth, and sun-bathed for a while before tottering off to find the first meal of spring. There was no competition for food, the earth providing more than enough for every tortoise to enjoy munching happily on the succulent new leaves.

Once we male tortoises had eaten our fill, though, there was plenty of competition for the favours of the females. For a while I simply watched and learned. I realised that it was by no means always the strongest male who won: a smaller tortoise, like me, could succeed in overturning a bigger rival. It's all in the angle of attack. By then, you see, I'd absorbed Pythagoras' theorem about angles and corresponding sides, and so I could turn the work of that great ancient Greek to my advantage. My chosen female had a very attractive shell which wasn't excessively domed. The underside of a male tortoise's shell is slightly concave, enabling him to mount the female successfully, but one doesn't want to make the process any more laborious than necessary, so a female with a less convex shell is attractive. And this particular female was *very* attractive. Still, I concentrated solely on my rival, and launched my attack at what I judged to be the best possible moment. Happily for me, it was. Using my Pythagoras-proven angle against my rival's corresponding side, I knocked him off-balance and sent him slithering down the grassy slope.

Meanwhile, the very attractive female just went on nibbling clover; females can be so coy. But she seemed to appreciate my song, and I called her Shelley, since the lines of her shell were pure poetry to me. So our mating was successful. Eventually. Then Shelley ambled off; in due season she would dig a suitable nest-hole to lay her eggs, while I could rest assured that I had produced my own heirs.

Throughout that second summer on the island I continued my peaceful existence, dividing my time between the productive earth and the ruins of the bipeds' temple, while continuing to absorb our culture and traditions. In addition to the knowledge handed down by Ptolemy the Greek Tortoise and gleaned from bipeds like Pythagoras, there were also those stories of ancient memories and fabled creatures, which I mentioned earlier. These were chronicled by an ancient Greek biped called Æsop, although I've often thought that Æsop himself probably wasn't a biped but a tortoise, since he taught-us all, chelonians and bipeds alike, to respect the great motto of all tortoises:

"Slow and steady wins the race."

Meanwhile, though, the warring bipeds were continuing their own, very bitter race: to win the whole of Greece. The devastation was spreading, along with the bipeds themselves, until they began to encroach on our hillside and disturb our time-honoured way of life. Nowadays, I believe the bipeds refer to such incursions into other species' territories as 'destruction of habitat', and shake their heads mournfully over the effects of their own actions on the natural world. But at that time there was no leisure to ponder such philosophical questions, even in Greece; it was quite simply destruction, and when the explosions started, just as they'd done in Morocco, the destruction escalated.

It escalated even further when one faction of the warring bipeds suddenly came swarming across our hill like overgrown ants; then the hill itself seemed to explode as a second faction attacked the first faction. Overhead, dark shapes swooped and dived from the sky like giant birds of prey, except that these monsters were roaring maniacally and spewing flames, too. I've since learned that some of them, at least, were of the genus *Spitfire*.

Escape now became imperative. The only option seemed to be to stow away once again, courtesy of the unsuspecting and preoccupied bipeds, and leave that formerly idyllic Greek island, in search of some other sanctuary.

It was at this point in my decision-making that I was rudely interrupted: there was an explosion much nearer than ever before. My hearing seemed to explode, too; my eyes hurt; and then the world went black. Not the gentle, restorative oblivion of hibernation, but a sudden, lurching descent into darkness, followed by – nothing.

Chapter 4: Marching Orders
On the migration of species

Shell shock is a very unpleasant condition, which isn't actually limited to those of us with shells. It can also be experienced by bipeds caught up in the trauma of warfare, despite their lacking any type of naturally protective shell. That is, unless you count the tiny pink shells on the ends of their fingers and toes, as baby bipeds are generally taught to do. The rest of us, though, prefer not to concern ourselves with the sequential progression of numbers in the way favoured by the bipeds: we simply rely on the natural order of things.

Anyway, that explosion had plunged me into severe shell shock, causing me to withdraw deep into myself as if into a sudden, unscheduled hibernation. But eventually I began to surface into consciousness once more, although there seemed to be some sort of very hot hammer at work inside my head. To add to my disorientation, the world around me was lurching in the same way as it had done in my private *Grenades* cabin during the sea-crossing to Greece. Evidently I was at sea again, but I could feel the side of a box against my shell, so at least I wasn't floating around in a ship's hold. So I must have left Greece, in a box which seemed to be of about the same size as the travelling-crate in which I'd first arrived there as a refugee from Morocco. But this box was lined with coarse sand rather than with metal imitation tortoises, which was a lot more comfortable than being balanced amongst all those shells with pins sticking out. Somehow it felt safer, too.

My private accommodation was suitably sheltered below decks, and judging by the seemingly endless vibrations of heavy biped feet tramping about, I had embarked on this next journey on a much larger ship. One particular biped was making frequent checks on me, crouching down beside my box and gently stroking my shell while making soothing noises. Instinct told me to remain withdrawn into myself for the time being, since my recent experiences had only served to remind me that trust between members of different species has to be earned, very gradually: particularly where bipeds are concerned. For now, I would need to reserve both my strength and my judgement until my new circumstances became a little clearer, since my life was evidently undergoing yet another sea change. But instinct also told me, as the naturalist Charles Darwin told the bipeds:

"It is not the strongest of the species that survives, nor the most intelligent, but the one most responsive to change."

That seems to sum up my own species very well. After all, I reflected, as I drifted off into a healing sleep, not only Greek tortoises but chelonians generally have been adept at colonization for centuries. In setting off into the unknown once more, I would simply be following in the distinctively clawed footsteps of my ancestors, and also of the various other members of the Chelonian Order who have travelled the world.

Charles Darwin himself became very involved with tortoises and migration, partly thanks to his long association with Harriet, a Galapagos Islands tortoise. Harriet had travelled to England to live with Charles

Darwin and assist him with his researches, passing on at least something of our ancient chelonian wisdom and undoubtedly helping him in his work on the origin of species. Harriet adapted very successfully to her new habitat, despite the shock of the climate change; from the warmth and sunshine of her own native island to the cool and damp of Charles Darwin's native island.

As bipeds have a much shorter lifespan than tortoises, Harriet thought nothing of outliving her biped companion. After Charles Darwin's death she continued to travel and to sample different climates, eventually going to live in Australia with another naturalist biped, called Steve Irwin, whose main interest was the study of crocodiles. Apart from being fellow reptiles, we tortoises really have nothing in common with crocodiles: we're calm, they're snappy. Personally I have no desire to meet a crocodile, as instinct warns me to steer well clear of any creature with such a perilous smile.

But naturalist bipeds don't always confine themselves to writing books about the rest of us: sometimes they like to get right in amongst us. Steve Irwin enjoyed spending time with crocodiles, despite their dangerous habit of popping out of the water when least expected, proving that even the most formidable species does have its champion. To be fair, though, it wasn't actually proximity to crocodiles which killed Steve Irwin, but a regrettable encounter with a stingray. He and Harriet died in the same year, but that's where the similarity ends: Steve Irwin died violently and young, whereas Harriet died peacefully and old, even by giant tortoise standards. She's

41

remembered as a great ambassador for the peaceful and adaptable chelonian way of life, and that's a fitting memorial to any tortoise.

In addition to Harriet, the Galapagos Islands are famous for other very important tortoises, both native and immigrant. After Harriet had travelled to England with Charles Darwin, another giant tortoise, called Jonathan, hitched a ride with some bipeds from his native Seychelles to St Helena in the Galapagos Islands. Perhaps Jonathan just wanted a change of scene, or maybe he shared Harriet's desire to see more of the world and become involved in the bipeds' evolutionary researches.

Whatever his reasons, Jonathan settled into his new habitat as easily as Harriet had done, and became famous for an admirable list of chelonian achievements. He was the first tortoise to have his photo taken and published, very soon after the bipeds had invented their art of photography. For this great event Jonathan posed nobly in the paddock in front of the St Helena Governor's house. He still lives in that same paddock, which seems an appropriate residence for such an old and venerable member of the local community.

Jonathan is also the first tortoise to have become actively involved in biped-style local government. Actively involved up to a point, that is, since he naturally remains true to our 'slow and steady' motto. But helping the bipeds in the running of local affairs – or, more accurately, in the ambling of local affairs – was obviously too good an opportunity for Jonathan to miss. His assistance has been invaluable because his position, both in his physical location and in his capacity as a senior member of the Chelonian Order of Reptiles, admirably fits him for bidding a ceremonious welcome and farewell to his island's succession of Governors and visiting dignitaries. On these occasions Jonathan stands in front of the official residence, tall and imposing as only a giant tortoise can be, and undeniably standing out from the crowd despite his lack of any biped-style official insignia. That wouldn't suit him at all, since a gold chain of office might easily become entangled round his front legs, and could prove limiting and possibly downright dangerous, even though he never condescends to descend the sweeping steps. Instead, Jonathan merely inclines his head in courteous acknowledgement of his biped counterparts. His presence gives these ceremonial occasions a reassuring air of permanence in a world of change, as though Jonathan were the official Head of State – rather than the unofficial one. At the very least, Jonathan's first official photograph, taken so long ago, must lend a certain dignity to the portrait gallery in the elegant hallway of the Governor's residence.

Away from his public duties, Jonathan likes to relax and forage in the grounds of the Governor's house. This naturally involves a certain amount of rather messy earth-moving, as is common to us tortoises whatever our size. However, Jonathan needs to look his clean and shiny best on public occasions, so he recently indulged in his first-ever bath: at his admittedly advanced age, a certain amount of grime had become ingrained in his impressively large shell. Being a giant tortoise and consequently rather heavy, even by biped standards, Jonathan is unable to bathe comfortably in the sort of modest plastic container in which I have often enjoyed a wallow, courtesy of my own bipeds. But Jonathan's bath attendant, however obliging, would find it difficult to hoist him over the rigid sides of any bath, so Jonathan actually settled for a shower, instead. He didn't even need the latest walk-in style: his obliging biped carefully poured water over his shell and then walked all around him, gently massaging away the dirt with a large but suitably soft scrubbing brush, before thoroughly rinsing his shell with clean water. Having himself been involved with photography practically since its invention, Jonathan graciously allowed a few photographers into his paddock for the occasion, and judging by his contented expression in yet another photo of this supremely photogenic tortoise, Jonathan evidently enjoyed his first experience of taking a modern shower.

Despite being naturally reticent, Jonathan didn't object to the fame which these photographs brought him. His experience had already taught him that publicity simply serves to bring the need for conservation to a wider biped audience. As he is officially the oldest living land animal ever recorded, and with there being only a few Seychelles tortoises left in the world, it's a comfort to know that Jonathan has proved to be such an excellent ambassador, carrying his fame with dignity. He has now been given his very own, full-time biped carer, a reward which he richly deserves.

So we chelonians are very adaptable, and this collective memory of our species' survival was particularly reassuring to me, as the bipeds' ship continued its seemingly unsteady course towards my next destination. But I certainly wasn't counting my hatchlings before they were hatched: apart from the fact that we tortoises don't count in the same way as bipeds do, our collective memory – otherwise known as instinct – also reminded me that even tortoises can't always be successful at responding to change.

As a case in point, I'm sure Charles Darwin would be very upset if he knew about the fate of yet another Galapagos Islands tortoise, called George, who is probably the most well-known of all tortoises as far as the bipeds are concerned. George became known by the bipeds as Lonesome George as he was the last of his subspecies. This unhappy circumstance came about because the vegetation on which George and his kind depended, and which was specific to their island, had been devastated by a particular type of goat. These goats were not native to that particular island, but had been brought in by…the bipeds. George became very famous when the bipeds tried to make amends for destroying his habitat, by finding a suitable mate for him. Unfortunately, though, it was too late; by the time the bipeds finally realised the consequences of having introduced the goats, there were no other tortoises of his subspecies left, apart from George himself.

But Lonesome George wasn't really lonely, in the way that bipeds understand loneliness, since we tortoises prefer to live solitary lives even when amongst our own kind. So the real tragedy of Lonesome George wasn't so much his own isolation – though I'm sure he would have liked a mate of his own subspecies, to satisfy the natural instinct to reproduce – as the fact that he was the last. George remains very famous amongst the bipeds, perhaps because the Galapagos tortoises are so large and impressive-looking. In fact, George has become a symbol of the need for preservation of habitat, and conservation efforts generally, not only in Galapagos but all over the world.

Another positive result of George's influence has been the re-population of a different Galapagos Island, by a male tortoise called Diego. He arrived from a comfortably settled home with the bipeds, who appear to have thought so highly of him that they must have named their local wildlife sanctuary in his honour: San Diego Zoo. Despite being of a venerable age himself, Diego has risen to the challenge of establishing his very own, enormously successful, breeding programme. Thanks to Diego's selfless efforts, his subspecies has been saved from extinction and is now re-established on its original island.

So the bipeds have traditionally done their best to help, by providing transport and habitat for various tortoises, as well as publicity. But the most unusual chelonian expedition of all was when a different set of bipeds – called Russians – took chelonian companions with them in their spacecraft, which was the first rocket to go all the way to the moon, travel right round it, and return to Earth. The tortoises on board each lost weight during their mission, which explains why they were more than ready for a decent meal once they'd touched down again. Just like Jonathan, these astronautical tortoises took the opportunity to publicize their participation in scientific research – in their case, space exploration.

After re-entry and with the cameras clicking, these tortoises tucked in heartily to a well-earned salad, showing their appreciation of the biped ground crew's thoughtfulness in standing by with the lettuce. Fortunately their extra-terrestrial weight loss had nothing to do with any biped-style exertion, but was merely due to the effects of being in space. These pioneering tortoises didn't, for instance, indulge in any space-walking excursions outside their spacecraft, which was very sensible as it would have been extremely difficult for them to wear the necessary oxygen tanks securely strapped to their domed shells. They didn't even need to wear goldfish bowls on their heads, as sported by their accompanying bipeds, since the astronauts had carefully provided more suitable airtight facilities for their tortoise counterparts: astronauts and astro-torts working in harmony.

These astro-torts were necessarily small, since giants like Harriet, Jonathan and George would undoubtedly have found conditions on board a space rocket rather uncomfortably cramped. Anyway, being elderly even by our standards, they might have become slightly traumatized at blast-off. But it was certainly a giant step for tortoisekind.

Mostly, though, we tortoises prefer to remain terrestrial when colonizing new territories. England has proved to be an especially popular destination, despite its unreliable climate. On the other forefoot, its damp climate does mean that the vegetation there is particularly succulent. England is part of the British Isles which, in addition to the water all around them, have a lot of water all over them, too. It often rains throughout the British Isles, which is surprising as I should have thought the place had enough water already, although this gives the biped inhabitants an endless topic of conversation; they are famous for talking about the weather. I began to wonder, fleetingly, whether I might be destined to settle there; after all, the voyage was most definitely lengthening out, and judging by the increased motion on board ship, we had evidently left my own home waters of the Mediterranean.

England would be an interesting next port of call, in any case. Its biped population is considered to be not only generally friendly, but perfectly willing to co-operate in providing suitable accommodation for its chelonian immigrants, such as the *vivarium*, complete with heat and sun lamps, set up much later by my own biped family. Of course, this type of indoor *vivarium* is a modern biped invention, which didn't exist when Charles Darwin's Harriet arrived. But Harriet wasn't the only tortoise to thrive in England's climate, and to achieve a modest degree of fame while doing so, even before the invention of the indoor *vivarium*.

Another famous English naturalist and willing chelonian host was Gilbert White, who lived in a Hampshire village called Selborne with Timothy, his tortoise companion. Timothy became almost as well-known as his biped, since he featured prominently in Gilbert White's journal which was published many years ago and is still famous nowadays. Not content with this, though, it seems that Timothy had dictated his own journal, which was eventually published as *Timothy's Book: Notes of an English Country*

Tortoise. The title of his memoirs just goes to prove how successfully we tortoises can become integrated into our adopted surroundings.

By coincidence, there was another tortoise called Timothy who also became famous, after he went to live at Powderham Castle in Devon. This Timothy arrived in England after discharging his responsibilities as a ship's mascot. He and his biped carer, who was a naval captain, had met the famous female biped Florence Nightingale, together with Jimmy, *her* tortoise companion. Jimmy, in turn, had spent several years in a military hospital during another of the bipeds' famous wars, cheering up the patients. So we tortoises do our best to help the bipeds, in return for their assistance with transport and colonization: that motto of the biped nobility, *noblesse oblige*, seems very suitable for the Chelonian Order of Reptiles, too.

The two Timothys – Selborne and Powderham – shared another coincidence: their respective biped carers assumed, wrongly, that each of them was male. Of course, the bipeds can't really be expected to understand the subtleties of shape and form in male and female tortoises' shells, as bipeds themselves only have those little shells at the ends of their limbs, but even so, it was a surprising mistake for any biped naturalist to make. After all, we tortoises can distinguish easily enough between male and female bipeds, and not only because the female of the species sometimes changes the colour of her little shells. My own research has shown that this phenomenon occurs primarily during the summer months, when the female's little shells can turn red, pink or purple.

Shades of blue or even green may also occur, which could be unfortunate if a passing tortoise should mistake her toes for an unusual but succulent-looking tuft of vegetation, or a tasty flower head, and start munching.

Anyway, it turned out that the two Timothys were, in fact, the two Timotheas, although each was always known as Timothy. Personally, I am without doubt a male tortoise, but I do feel a certain affinity for both the Timothys, having followed in their footsteps to some extent. Like each of them, I had left my Mediterranean home on board ship, in the company of the bipeds...

Chapter 5: Wavelengths
A voyage of discovery

While I was musing gently on this seemingly endless stream of conscious colonization, and dreaming of my own evolving part in it, the effects of shell shock were gradually subsiding. This was due partly to the deep sleep I was enjoying in my sand-lined box, and partly to the regular rehydration treatment being administered by an obliging biped, who seemed to be providing me with the kind of nursing care of which Florence Nightingale and Jimmy would have been proud. When I first felt recovered enough to protrude my head a little, my eyes felt sticky as I tried to open them. My next sensation was a soft, cool wetness on my eyelids as they were being gently wiped. Then a biped hand came into slightly hazy focus, and a wave of relief swept over me, along with the wave of cool water clearing my eyes: I still had my sight, as well as my hearing. Next, I felt water being drizzled softly over my shell, soothing and rehydrating me at the same time, while the quiet biped voice continued in its reassuring tone. I began to sense that I had somehow fallen into company with one of those biped naturalists who know something about tortoises, like Harriet and the Timothys before me.

Cautiously, once my head began to clear, I decided to be bold and stick my neck out further, if only to try to work out where I was. As I continued to rouse slowly and steadily from my stupor, and felt inclined to stick my neck out increasingly often, more of this obliging biped came into view. His battle-stained khaki bore various markings, which were probably as individual to him as the markings on my shell are to me. More importantly, his battle-weary face bore the marks of experiences which had, all too obviously, been similar to my own.

As the sea became rougher, this obliging biped brought me some sort of soft padding to make my accommodation on board more comfortable, since my involuntary movement inside the box was becoming more pronounced and more difficult to control. I appreciated his gesture very much, though I remained cautious, with instinct still warning me to beware. But the gentle care provided by this biped continued, despite my lack of response, and in fact his visits became more frequent as the ship rose and fell on an increasingly heavy swell. As his own physical discomfort evidently increased with the pitching and rolling of the ship, and his own mental stresses just as evidently continued to trouble him, this soldiering biped appeared to derive increasing comfort from his concern for me and his consequent efforts on my behalf.

The result of all this was that a natural empathy began to develop between us, as the voyage lengthened out and the soldiering biped spent increasing amounts of time in my company, so that I began to regard him as my very own, seafaring not-so-petty officer. As that empathy grew towards a mutual trust, I began to recognise his footsteps and found it unnecessary to withdraw into my shell at his approach. He, for his part, would bring me such titbits as he could find on board – mainly cabbage stalks and apple cores from the galley – as my appetite began to revive. While I ate, slowly and methodically, he would speak softly about his home in a green valley in a place called Cornwall which, as I later learned, juts out into the sea to form the very tip of England. From the weary longing in his tone of voice, and the gentleness of his hand as he bathed my shell, I began to feel that perhaps this valley in Cornwall might be an ideal destination for a wandering tortoise. The climate sounded generally acceptable: though perhaps sometimes a little on the damp side (even by English standards), it was apparently mild and even relatively warm, with good bouts of sunshine to encourage the growth of rich and varied vegetation. Apparently Cornwall even possessed some palm trees, so it couldn't be too bad.

I gleaned all this fresh and illuminating knowledge from that increasing ability to communicate, which develops out of sheer necessity when two members of different species find themselves together in a situation of common danger, or simply of shared discomfort. But biped communication is much more complex than the chelonian version, or any other creature's version, come to that. Unlike the rest of us, the bipeds rely mainly on a particular form of vocal communication, which is extremely complicated. But this reliance on speech tends to mean that the bipeds do sometimes lack that subtlety of communication, by instinctive body language, which various other species have developed to a far higher degree. As well as talking to each other, bipeds tend to talk instinctively to other creatures as an integral part of forming a bond with them, to the extent that some mammals can learn to understand biped words quite easily. Dogs and horses are particularly good at understanding a whole range of speech patterns, due to their constant interaction with the bipeds. In my own case, I found that with a lot of practice and the patience natural to my species, it became possible to learn how to infer meaning from my particular biped's intonation and phrasing, and eventually from some of his individual words. This was principally because I had plenty of opportunities to refine my own perceptions and develop my own understanding, during those days of close companionship with my soldiering biped as that wartime sea-crossing was setting the next course of my life.

While the ship forged onwards into what were, for me at least, uncharted waters, the sea became uncomfortably rough, and then the noise became uncomfortably loud as the ship was attacked by the other biped faction. The water churned and crashed against the sides of the ship, which would lurch violently and then seem to shudder anew, from the noise and vibration of its own weapons being fired. I took the opportunity to withdraw into my shell once again. But my biped continued his regular visits to check on me, always speaking to me in that same quiet, reassuring tone, and telling me of the green pastures that awaited us both in Cornwall, when the turmoil of warfare should finally be over.

The bipeds have an additional way of communicating, which is unique to them, and this was another fact which became apparent while my soldiering biped and I were confined on our war-tossed ship. He would produce from his pocket a small sheaf of papers, attached to each other along one long side and bound together inside a protective covering. The bipeds call this a book, which is part of their extensive system of storing the knowledge which they've collectively accumulated over time. My biped would look at the book, making sense of the black marks on its white pages so that the thoughts stored inside the book became accessible to him. Then he would speak parts of it aloud so that, little by little, the information inside the book became accessible to me, too. When he had delved sufficiently into the pages of one small book, usually over the course of several sessions spent sitting beside my travelling-box, my biped would start afresh the next time with another one.

Once I'd managed to work all this out, during those long periods of solitude which are perfectly natural to us tortoises and provide ample time to absorb new information, I became fascinated by this novel idea. Some books are actually called 'novels', but I soon learned that this particular biped loved all sorts of books, as he would read from them on a variety of subjects, some of which were more relevant to my case than others, of course. He appeared to like nothing better than to read these extracts to me in his spare time, so I began to encourage him as much as possible, by sticking my neck out with my head slightly on one side, just to show him that I was listening, and letting my concentration show in my wide-open eyes and, I hoped, my intent expression.

All this was a completely new way of absorbing information, as far as I was concerned. It soon became a very absorbing hobby, too, and one which I've continued to enjoy ever since my time on board that ship. Personally, though, I've never had any desire to embark on learning to read for myself: after all, why keep a biped and embark yourself?

In any case, I think that gleaning knowledge from the various bipeds and their books must be quite an unusual hobby for a tortoise. We in the animal kingdom generally prefer to rely on instinct, that communal fund of each species' knowledge as it constantly evolves through successive generations, to ensure that life remains viable as environment and experience change. So our thinking is purely intuitive, and our knowledge is written deep inside us, from the very start of life. The bipeds' fund of knowledge, by contrast, is so complex and so vast that any one individual of the species can't possibly be expected to remember all of it. Even though bipeds have much larger brains than anyone else (a fact which causes bipeds generally to feel very proud of themselves, and to flatter themselves as being distinctly superior to the rest of us), this means that they need to store knowledge somewhere outside their brains, so that it can be shared amongst them.

Those ancient Greek bipeds, with whom we tortoises share so much of our cultural history, were some of the first to develop a system for storing and transferring their knowledge. While we tortoises were happily basking, gradually absorbing the necessary knowledge along with the equally necessary sunshine, the Greek bipeds were preserving their knowledge in book form. Not just the Greeks, but various bipeds all around the world had begun gradually transcribing their knowledge in a similar way, by marking white sheets with a series of squiggly black lines to represent their thoughts and their speech patterns.

This system of writing became very effective, and is very similar to the modern bipeds' writing, except that the white sheets aren't rolled up any more in the way that the ancient versions were. Nowadays they use smaller pages bound into books, which is a much more efficient system, and easier to use. Certainly it would have been almost impossible for my soldiering biped to unroll an ancient-style scroll in the confines of our quarters aboard that ship, quite apart from the discomfort he would have experienced when trying to carry a scroll around in a pocket of his uniform.

The bipeds study all sorts of subjects in this way, and even write books about the rest of us. Given all the work done by the biped naturalists with the assistance of various tortoises, it wasn't really a surprise when I learned from my own biped that tortoises have featured in several books, and not only written by naturalists, either. My soldiering biped, for instance, seemed particularly fond of an author called George Eliot, and took great delight in reading aloud to me one particular passage written by this author, because it was about a tortoise. The tortoise in the book is described as being a stray, so it must have been in a similar predicament to mine on board that war-tossed ship. Unusually for one of our species, though, that particular tortoise seemed to lack any sense of purpose or direction, as it was described as dangling about and being of desultory pursuits. My biped seemed to find this almost as upsetting as I did: he dwelt on those words for some considerable time, repeating the phrases and shaking his head. He went on to read that the same tortoise eventually decided to 'protrude its small head ambitiously and become rampant.' Regarding me with a developing understanding, and gently stroking my shell, this thoughtful biped then wondered aloud how I, being a tortoise most definitely *not* of desultory pursuits, could possibly have found my way into the midst of that battle between the biped factions for control of a Greek island. He seemed to wish that my growing understanding of his speech patterns could somehow be reciprocated. But that, of course, remains an impassable divide, as ordained by nature itself: our collective knowledge is safely stored away at the core of our being. And so my biped was left to wonder, while I kept to myself the story of how I had crossed the sea once already, found a new home, and thrived there for several years.

By this stage in the voyage, I'd learned enough to realise that my next port of call was, indeed, to be England: the adopted homeland of Harriet and the Timothys. I found myself hoping that no one in England would make the same mistake as had happened to the Timothys, as I didn't really want to become Jemima or Geraldine. My soldiering biped had already started calling me Jerry, although that wasn't actually my original name, back in Greece. I don't really remember having a particular name of my own, in my early days, so Jerry has done very well for me, ever since the beginning of my association with my English bipeds. In fact, I was already becoming used to hearing my name, and I didn't really relish the idea of changing it, 'specially for a name more appropriate to a female.

But this apparently casual substitution of male for female names is another trait which I've noticed amongst the bipeds, quite apart from the case of the Timothys. For instance, I gradually understood that my soldiering biped's favourite author, George Eliot, wasn't really a male biped called George Eliot, but a female biped called Mary Ann Evans. Through my long association with the English bipeds and their books, I've also learned of a very famous family of female bipeds who wrote books under the names of Currer, Ellis and Acton Bell, to disguise the fact that they were female. It all seems rather complicated, to me: I think their original names of Charlotte, Emily and Anne Brontë were just as good, and avoided any confusion.

Whether male or female, George Eliot clearly hadn't consulted Mr Darwin, or any of the other naturalists, before writing about rampant tortoises. Speaking for myself, on board that ship, I wouldn't have wanted to risk moving about outside my travelling-box at all, but in any case, we tortoises prefer not to be rampant, particularly when suffering from shell shock: over-activity is anathema to any tortoise, as it completely contradicts our 'slow and steady' motto.

Neither do we adopt the rampant attitude favoured by mediaeval bipeds, when depicting various creatures of noble mien on their banners and shields. These were usually pictures of mammals such as lions and unicorns rather than reptiles such as tortoises, probably because in mediaeval times, tortoises hadn't yet spread rampantly throughout Europe. Though I rather doubt whether lions or unicorns had, either. But any tortoise would find it uncomfortable, if not impossible, to pose on the hind legs while waving the forefeet in the air: the resultant overbalancing would be bound to lead to a very serious case of shell shock. All of which is a great pity, since the profile of a heraldic tortoise – as a proud representative of the Chelonian Order of Reptiles – would undoubtedly have looked distinctly noble, emblazoned on a flag or painted on one of those glass pictures in the windows of an important building. I'm sure Jonathan, that noble island-governing tortoise, would approve.

However, my own reality on board that ship was very different from any sort of imagined heraldic nobility. The attacks from the other biped faction eventually subsided into an uneasy calm, while the pitching and rolling of the ship increased. Neither situation was ideal, but we chelonians can be as stoical as any ancient Greek. Throughout, my obliging biped still visited me as often as he could. When we entered calmer waters and the general turmoil around us seemed to recede, I began to sense that the voyage must be nearly over. The tramp of feet on the deck above me increased, to the accompaniment of thumps as boxes and bags were hauled out on deck. Then my own biped appeared again, followed by another, younger version who addressed him as 'Sir' and referred to my travelling-box as 'the Major's prize possession'. A box load of coarse sand didn't strike me as being any great prize, but by now I was learning to trust the judgement of Sir-or-the-Major. I felt that 'the Major' suited him.

Our ship finally docked at a naval base, which I later learned was called Devonport. The whole place seemed to be engulfed in frenetic activity and noise, coming at us in a confusing mass from the sea, from the land and even from the air. This was on a much larger scale than my arrival on that small Greek island, and I was very glad that this time I had no need to make my own way out of the port, being safely lodged inside my travelling-box. More travelling followed, in a long line of lurching carriages crowded with bipeds, all the carriages being pulled by a noisy machine at the front which poured smoke as it rocketed along. Once again, I withdrew further into my shell, glad that the lid of my travelling-box was firmly closed. Then I felt the box being moved once more: loaded onto a cart this time, where I bounced slightly on my bed of sand as the clip-clopping of a horse's hooves took over from the smelly, smoking machine.

Finally, my box was lifted down, carried a short distance, and then I was being gently helped out by biped hands, onto a sweet-smelling green pasture with familiar dandelions and clover, alongside other plants as yet unknown to me. But I had arrived: this must be Cornwall.

Chapter 6: Eden projected
Savouring a Cornish pasture

I'd already learned quite a lot about Cornwall, from
the Major's musings on board our ship. In addition to
palm trees and lush vegetation, Cornwall possesses
some spectacular and very steep cliffs (I immediately
made a mental note to avoid those), plus its own
biped food called Cornish pasties and chelonian food
called Cornish pastures. Just as importantly, from a
pastoral point of view, Cornwall has the mildest and
sunniest climate in Great Britain. Sticking out into the
sea at the tip of England, it looks very much like a
tortoise's tail, being rather stubby in shape and with a
distinctly rugged surface.

Cornwall's biped population seems to consider the
place as being almost entirely separate, probably
because it's pretty much surrounded by water, what
with the sea and a river which forms most of
Cornwall's border with the rest of England. The
Cornish bipeds even have their own ancient form of
speech, although it's not used much, either nowadays
or even when I first arrived. This was very fortunate
for me at the time, as I was concentrating all my
efforts on understanding the Major's English speech,
and I'm not sure how I could have coped if he'd
suddenly launched into Cornish. Cornwall also has its
own flag, of which the resident bipeds seem very
proud, although to be honest, I think its white cross
on a black background is a bit on the plain side, and
doesn't do justice to Cornwall's gloriously productive
pastures. It would definitely be cheered up by the

addition of a heraldic tortoise, perhaps shown above a pair of crossed dandelions.

Having arrived in England during that turbulent time when the entire population seemed to be traumatised by biped warfare, I began to take stock of my new and blissfully peaceful surroundings. As I discovered more about this green Cornish valley, I came to realise that I'd fetched up in a place which was just as worthy of heraldic devices as Jonathan's residence outside the Governor's house, on that distant island of St Helena. The Major's family had lived in this same place for generations, and I soon learned to appreciate why.

The Major's ancestors had built themselves a large and impressive-looking house, standing in its own well-stocked gardens with fields and woods beyond. The whole place was called Treshillick; lots of Cornish place names start with *Tre*, as the Major said it means that the inhabitants feel at home there. That's the only Cornish word the Major ever taught me, but it seemed to bode well for my new abode. Personally, though, I think a mistake had been made when the bipeds first wrote it down, and it should really have been called Tre*shell*ick, since it provided sheltered accommodation for its bipeds, and pastures perfectly suited to the chelonian lifestyle. Treshellick would seem to be a more appropriate name as far as the Major himself was concerned, too, because in addition to being very fond of his native Cornwall, he'd now proved himself to be very fond of a refugee tortoise.

On being helped down from the cart and out of my travelling-box, I found myself at the edge of a gently sloping and pleasantly sunny pasture, where it bordered a rose garden laid out to one side of Treshillick House itself. The scents wafting on a slight breeze promised a rich variety of succulent vegetation, while shade was provided by an old oak tree standing in the middle of this modestly-sized but evidently well-stocked meadow. Several bipeds, led by a female of about the same age as the Major, had come running from the house to greet him. Their relief and joy hung palpably in the air, during their long moment of reunion. I left them to it, and stepped carefully through the stone archway in the wall which divided the cultivated rose garden from the wild pasture. From there, I began making my way along the edge of the meadow, since we tortoises like to get the measure of our surroundings by first walking all around the perimeter of any enclosure.

The wall separating the meadow from the rose garden was high and evidently very old, being made of mellowed stone. This would be a perfect place to bask on summer days, with my shell propped comfortably against the sun-warmed stone. Turning myself round to look back, I could see the Major and his female still standing together in a silent embrace, their figures framed by that open archway in the wall, and silhouetted against the view beyond. Content to leave them exactly as they stood, I turned once more to my own affairs and a proper assessment of my surroundings.

The house itself was approached by a long driveway, along which the horse and cart must have clattered with my travelling-box. Pausing again, I could see that the gravel surface of this drive was flanked by short, springy turf, as it meandered uninterrupted through a sheltering belt of trees and into a hazy green distance. Beyond the trees could be glimpsed a series of gently sloping grassy mounds, which, as I later learned, had something to do with the ancient Cornish bipeds: probably their version of the ancient Greek bipeds' temples, though inevitably rain-drenched rather than sun-drenched, in this northern climate.

As it dipped towards the house, the drive threaded its way between velvety-green verges, while the ground-level lushness was overspread by a cascade of colour from the bushes which grew tall and strong in their fertile home: there would be springtime blossoms in all sorts of delicate shades, followed by strong, vivid early summer blooms and then softest pink wild roses to scent my favourite season, and finally the glowing red and orange heralds to signal the onset of autumn and preparation for hibernation.

Like the ancient Greeks, these Cornish builders must have been very fond of symmetry. The house was in the classical biped style, its white pillars emphasised by pale yellow walls and buff stonework, with formal gardens laid out in front and to the sides. These, in turn, gave onto meadows and then the woods beyond. The house stood in a perfectly rounded dell, the ground rising gently on all sides, so that from my pasture I could view its entire frontage, as if looking onto a juvenile biped's toy house. From one of my favourite vantage points, peering out from amongst the meadow grasses, I always felt that it should be possible to unhinge the whole front of the house, opening it to reveal all the typical biped bustle going on inside, as if on a miniature scale.

For now, though, any further study of the bipeds and their ways would have to wait, as I needed to establish my own residence in this idyllic and very English setting. Left to my own devices, I soon realised that this particular pasture would provide a perfectly suitable environment for me. The mellow wall divided it from the formal gardens along one side before giving way to a stretch of hedgerow, while in front of me the view opened onto fields stretching away beyond the bank of a shallow stream.

Coming from the Mediterranean, I was naturally very concerned about the English weather, so finding adequate shelter was a high priority for me. But that hedgerow offered plenty of scope for a small but determined tortoise to scrape out a suitable shelter for hibernation. I conducted a test dig, which proved that the earth was pleasantly pliable, while there would be an abundance of leaf mould during the autumn, and the hedge itself would provide adequate protection from wind and storms. Contented, I now gave my full attention to the food supply. The meadow supported a satisfying range of grasses, dandelions and plantains, mixed with juicy clover and a variety of wild flowers, including strawberry plants, all of which would provide a rich variety of seasonal treats. I paused to sample some of these culinary delights, before moving on to investigate the local water supply, making my way down the gently sloping, grassy bank towards the stream. The water was clear and cool, and not too deep or fast-flowing for me to drink safely. At the edges of the stream, dancing gently in the water, grew the tastiest treat of all: richly succulent watercress.

Making my way further along the bank of the stream – very slowly now, as by this time I was feeling rather full – I came to another sunny enclosure, bordering mine but fenced by closely-constructed wire. This discovery quickened my senses: amongst the scents of mixed grasses and some of Cornwall's most tropical vegetation, was the unmistakable smell of chelonian habitation. Sticking my neck out further as the inhabitants turned towards me, I could see that they were indeed tortoises. But these were not of my own, Greek subspecies: their distinctive markings showed them to be Indian Star tortoises. The shell of this type of tortoise is covered with radiating star-shaped markings, in shades of gold against a dark-coloured background, which gives them a very dramatic appearance. In their native land, these tortoises are considered as true jewels in the Indian crown. In Cornwall they are evidently given equally regal status, as I later learned that the Cornish bipeds named a village after them, or at least after the female of the species: Indian Queens is situated not far from the Treshillick estate.

Instinct warned me that these Indian Stars don't socialise with other types of tortoise. So I thanked my own lucky stars for that fence between us, having no desire to be bowled over on my back: a potentially unpleasant result of being Star-struck. But, having turned to assess me and deciding that I posed no threat to them, they resumed their peaceful grazing in their tropical garden, clearly content with their habitat and with life in general. Looking beyond this group of star-studded chelonians, I could see the purpose-built shelter which the members of such a delicate subspecies would certainly require, in order to survive in this northern climate. Clearly, then, the Major knew quite a lot about tortoises.

I made my way back up the gentle slope beside the Indian tortoises' fence, to complete this circumnavigation of my own new world. Next, I set off for the old oak tree at its centre, making my way towards my goal in a steady, straight line. It was well worth the effort. Already in its full summer leaf, the tree provided a large pool of gloriously dappled shade. Having by now nibbled my fill, I settled down comfortably and slipped into a peaceful doze, lulled by the meadow's scents and sounds.

It was a scent rather than a sound, though, which eventually woke me. Making slow, steady progress towards me through the grasses was another tortoise, and evidently a female, from the scent wafting ahead of her on a gentle current of air. But this was no Indian Queen; this was a member of my own subspecies, another true *testudo graeca*. She approached warily, emanating curiosity; then, as my strong male scent reached her, she stopped. The mating season being over for that year, we merely sized each other up, not moving in too close. After all, we Greek tortoises respect our own and each other's territories, only coming together when instinct tells us to mate. The meadow was more than large enough to accommodate us both, but I was relieved to be sharing my pastures with a female, rather than another male: far less stressful. So she and I parted company amicably enough, secure in the natural promise of our pairing next spring.

Beyond the oak tree, near the old wall, I now noticed a rather strange structure, humped in amongst the foliage like an enormous, semi-recumbent tortoise. I approached warily, in my turn, emanating as much curiosity as my recent female companion, but I could detect no scent, and no movement. Gradually I realised that this was no living creature, but some sort of biped-built dugout. I gave it a few hard nudges, just to make sure it was harmless, and then investigated further by walking all around it, since it was far too solid for me to walk straight through it, as I would instinctively have preferred to do. At one end of this oval-shaped mound I did find an opening, but I was glad to see that it was protected by a slightly raised step, to prevent any passing creature from falling inside. Placing my front legs on this step, I stood up on tip-claws so that I could peer in. The inside of this dugout was dark, cool and empty. Presumably the bipeds had decided to establish some form of tortoise-style protection for themselves, but against what? After all, they had that large house, just on the other side of the wall and the gardens.

At this point in my musings, I was interrupted by the sound of approaching bipeds.

"Cor, look – it's another tortoise, just like the Major told us!"

I felt small biped hands closing around my shell, and then a different young voice called out:

"Leave 'un alone! You know they'm creatures don't want picking up!"

I felt myself being released. Recovering my balance and regaining the safety of all four legs (standing on tip-claws is not the easiest position to maintain, with or without the assistance of biped hands), I saw two biped figures leaning towards me. These were evidently juveniles of the species, but I withdrew into my shell as a matter of course, and waited to see what would happen next.

They settled themselves comfortably in the grass beside me, and I felt a small hand cautiously stroking my shell. Then a familiar tread announced the arrival of the Major, still accompanied by his female. I protruded my head a little. They too sat down in the grass, the Major telling the juveniles a little about my lifestyle and habits. As usual when the Major was speaking, I concentrated all my efforts on understanding his meaning.

The Major's explanation of my situation led him to draw parallels with the situation of one of the two juveniles. The one who had spoken first, in a voice of such excitement as he bent forward and wanted to pick me up, was a newcomer to Treshillick, like me. He had been sent to Cornwall from his home in a far-off city, when the other warring biped faction had once again launched bombs; fast, flying bombs which whined through the air before landing on England's biggest city in a storm of fire and destruction. So all the juvenile bipeds had been sent away from the city: 'evacuated', the Major called it.

"So you see, Bob, you and Jerry are both evacuees; you, from London, and Jerry, from Greece."

Bob stroked my shell again.

"Will Jerry be going away then, like me, when the war's over?"

I listened intently to catch the Major's reply:

"You'll want to go home, won't you, Bob; you and your sister? But no, Jerry won't be going anywhere after the war: his only home's here, now."

I missed what was said next, in my relief at the prospect of staying in this peaceful, green valley.

"... but if they'm doodlebugs can't reach us down 'ere in Cornwall, Major, why do we still need the Anderson shelter?"

That was the other juvenile speaking, in a voice which would become known to me as the soft, Cornish accent. Patiently, the Major explained that the shelter had been built at the start of the war: as he was speaking, I gradually realised that he was referring to the dugout beside us. So my assumption had been right, and the dugout was yet another version of the bipeds' tortoise-style protection against attack. But I'd never learned about any tortoise called Anderson.

Satisfied, the two juveniles ran off: the Major's female had reminded them that it was nearly teatime, and they would be expected in the big kitchen at the house, where the mother of George the Cornish boy would be waiting for them. The Major lingered a while with his female and then, satisfied that I was well settled and provided for, he rose, taking her hand as they strolled together across the grass in the lengthening shadows.

Bob and George returned after their meal – I was still enjoying mine, the Cornish clover being particularly succulent as summer ripened to full abundance – bringing with them a female biped of about their own age. She made a great fuss of me, stroking my shell and saying some very nice things about its pattern. George, who must have been talking to the Major at teatime, was telling her about where I'd come from and the different plants I like to eat, with a note of pride in his voice. The female biped now spoke up, sounding rather awed:

"So Jerry's a sort of evacuee, like me an' Bob?"

"*Just* like us, Rosie!" called Bob triumphantly, scrambling up to go capering about the grass. George joined him, and the two of them were soon rolling around on the grass in mock-battle, just like juvenile male tortoises, though definitely looser-limbed and a lot more manoeuvrable in their play than I had ever been. But Rosie remained sitting on the grass beside me, oblivious to the noise of the two males, and still thoughtfully stroking my shell.

"The Major said he's been reading to you, Jerry. I'd like to read to you, too. That other tortoise, the one who looks like you, she keeps wandering off, but *we* can be friends."

I rather liked the sound of that. I knew from the Major that the bipeds set great store by education and breeding, which they view as being central to any civilised society. But education and breeding – particularly breeding – are naturally just as important to us chelonians as to bipeds. Here, in the peace and plenty of Cornwall, it seemed that I would be able to achieve both, at my own steady pace. I would be free to continue my education in science, geography, natural history and even in the bipeds' reading of books. And those gentle lines of Shelley's, which had proved unforgettable in that tortoise colony on a Greek hillside, could be repeated here in a Cornish garden – even if my new female turned out to have no taste for the natural poetry of my mating song.

Chapter 7: Hedge fund
Biped and chelonian bonds

Having very soon decided that I was going to like living in Cornwall, I spent the remainder of that summer busily mastering the art of balancing instinct with convenience. Busily in tortoise fashion, that is, as I checked on the progress and succulence of the various crops in my meadow. This is always a slow, meticulous process and, incidentally, a very tasty one.

I soon found the best basking places, too: my mornings were spent comfortably propped against the old stone wall whilst I recharged my personal solar-powered batteries, before making the daily tour of my domain, checking boundaries and sniffing for any scent of unwelcome visitors. Lunchtime would find me rootling happily amongst the crops growing in the meadow or at the edge of the stream. The languid afternoons were generally spent in the dappled shade under the oak tree, dozing peacefully after my morning's work in the field. After a light tea I would go for my regular evening walk, stopping now and then to enjoy a shaft of late sunshine on my shell. Finally, I would choose a comfortable spot for the night, beneath a convenient bush or snuggled comfortably amongst the remnants of last year's leaves under the hedge.

My new surroundings allowed me to maintain my independent way of life, with plenty of scope to forage for myself. The stream proved to be an unexpected source of delight, too: not only for its constant supply of good drinking water, but even for the occasional wallow in its shallows on hot afternoons, when the Cornish sun can be surprisingly strong. I would wade a little way into the water, then lower myself carefully, spreading my legs till the underside of my shell could rest comfortably on the bed of the stream so the cool water could flow gently all around me. On really hot days I'd extend my tail too, and even my neck, so that I could dip my head underwater for a long moment and bathe my eyes. Feeling refreshed, I would clamber out again from my own bespoke hydrotherapy pool, via the watercress swirling enticingly in the gentle eddies at the edge of the stream. Then I'd make my way towards one of my favourite basking places, and settling down comfortably to snooze, I would see again those pictures stored away inside my mind, of all the basking places I'd enjoyed in North Africa and in Greece. My new home was cooler, certainly, but we chelonians are traditionally adaptable, and Cornwall could meet all my summertime needs perfectly adequately.

Between the Major and my new young friend Rosie, I was never short of biped conversation whenever I wanted a little company. The Major continued to visit me in my sunny pasture as often as he could. Although he liked to busy himself around the grounds of Treshillick, he would still seek me out in the dappled afternoon shade underneath the oak tree, where he liked to pull one of his little books from a pocket and read aloud, sitting with his back resting against the trunk. I don't think he ever forgot our time together on board that ship, and the bond which had been forged then, between two disparate creatures in common distress, gave him continuing comfort during his respite from the horrors of warfare.

The juvenile bipeds seemed to take great delight in visiting me, too. But I think the young males were mostly interested in my pastures, really; they would chase bright butterflies and buzzing insects among the meadow grasses, or run down to the water and pull off their sandshoes to go splashing about in midstream with fishing nets, laughing and calling to each other. I don't think they ever managed to catch anything, though; the fish understood the game too well for that.

Rosie was much quieter. She would seek me out and sit down beside me, kicking off her shoes to wriggle her toes luxuriously in the grass. She kept her promise of reading to me, bringing much larger books than the Major had ever done. Her wide straw hat pulled down to shade her eyes as she read, Rosie would lie on her front facing me – she seemed to like reading to me face to face – with her elbows in the grass, her chin in her hands, and the book lying open on the grass between us. This meant that I had to look at the book upside down, but we both knew that didn't actually matter very much. I would extend my neck to rest my head in the sweet-smelling grass, while Rosie would read her favourite parts of the book aloud to me, sometimes laughing and sometimes saddened by what she read, but always asking my opinion:

"Oh, Jerry, how could Pooh Bear be so *silly*? But I do love him! Poor Eeyore, it's his birthday, and no one's brought him a present yet..."

"D'you think Brer Rabbit's going to be caught, this time? We've got our very own Briar Patch too, Jerry, here in your field!"

And so she would read on, whether it was one of her favourite animal stories, or a biped tale like Rapunzel imprisoned in her tower or Heidi running through her meadow. And always, at the most exciting part of the story, Rosie's knees would bend in the grass so that her feet would shoot up behind her, lower legs dancing a jig in the air as she lost herself in those word-pictures. I liked to think that she enjoyed my company as much as I enjoyed hers, throughout the remains of that idyllic summer in the meadow.

The inhabitants of Treshillick seemed to settle down to life in its allotted rhythms, as summer wore on and all the crops, for bipeds and chelonians alike, swelled to full ripeness under the benign Cornish sun. But just as I was comfortably settled into this peaceful new existence, I found that the world was about to change yet again, for myself and my biped companions.

As summer drew towards its close, I knew that warfare was looming again for the Major. I could feel the tension in his fingers when, running his hand over my shell one day and tracing its patterns with even more precision than usual, he told me that the he must soon return to Devonport, and from there to the war in the Mediterranean. He spoke to me of his longing to spend the winter in Cornwall, just as he used to do before the war: running the estate office and immersing himself in the working life of Treshillick; going for bright, crisp walks with his female companion and coming home to get warm again with tea at their fireside; curling up in the evenings to read books, with a pleasant glass of something to hand.

That all sounded fine for a biped, of course, and I disliked the idea of his going back to the biped war, probably almost as much as he did. Although it would mean his return to the gentler, warmer winter of the Mediterranean, he and I both knew from our shared experience that biped warfare takes no account of gentleness or warmth, anywhere. Instinct told me it would be better for all of us to stay here. Rosie and Bob, at least, were to spend that winter in Cornwall, as it wasn't yet considered safe for juvenile bipeds to return to England's biggest city: even the bipeds' tortoise-style Anderson shelters wouldn't protect them from the flying bombs being launched against them by the other biped faction.

As summer turned to autumn, I began to learn just how damp Great Britain can be. Rainfall and general dampness are only to be expected to some extent, quite naturally, as the place has water all around its edges. Less naturally, in my experience of islands, this one also has an unnecessary amount of water all over it. Especially in Cornwall. Not just in the rivers and reservoirs, but quite often sloshing about all over the fields and gardens, too, and sometimes even pouring along the roads.

As I began to conduct full-scale excavations for my *hibernaculum*, the ground immediately beyond my sheltering hedgerow was starting to become soggy. I had taken to spending every night underneath the hedgerow, burrowing my way in amongst the dried fallen leaves. When even these began to get a bit damp, the Major brought soft hay which he pushed in beneath the thickest part of the hedge so that I could shelter comfortably, untroubled by wind and rain. He also brought a barrowful of straw to spread across the ground immediately beyond the hedge, so that I could walk easily from the shelter of the hedgerow to the drier parts of the meadow near the old wall, where the last dandelions and plantains still enticed me to forage.

Sometimes Rosie would come to the hedgerow to watch me at work in the soft earth. In her over-large raincoat and shiny rubber boots, peering out from beneath the brim of her huge, borrowed rain hat, she would stand with her hands plunged deep into her coat pockets, or crouch down beside me and exclaim over the ever widening and deepening hole I was making. Every now and then I would pause in my work, and ease my shell into the hole to test its size and shape. This seemed to delight Rosie:

"Oh, Jerry, you look like you're swimming! And now you're making sure you can fit snugly inside, or maybe you're going to carry on and make your very own Heffalump Pit, just like Pooh Bear! I wish you could spend the winter indoors with me, but the Major says we must let you dig…"

Then, crouching down after a glance around her to make sure no one was watching, Rosie plucked me gently from the earth and picked me up, clutching me to her through the earth spattering my shell and the rain splattering her coat.

"I'll miss you, Jerry – see you in the spring," she whispered, and set me gently down again to continue my digging.

At about the same time, the morning came when the Major had to leave Treshillick and return to the war in the Mediterranean, as he'd already warned me. He came to say goodbye to me, close beside the hedgerow in the field which was only a part of his home, but which now comprised all of mine. Crouching down to stroke my shell as he'd done so many times before, the Major spoke to me as softly as ever, though perhaps not quite as easily: there was a tension in his voice as he told me about his plans for Treshillick, once the war was over.

Finally the Major stood up to leave, and strode purposefully back towards the old stone wall. I climbed out of my half-dug *hibernaculum* and followed him at my own pace, determined to see him on his way. I settled down to wait, watching from the archway in the wall between the meadow and the rose garden beside the house: between my world and his. Eventually the Major came out of the house, once more wearing his military khaki with its various markings. He turned to embrace his female, enfolding her completely in his arms, her head resting on his shoulder.

That view of the Major remains imprinted on my memory even now, after so many years: standing with his female on the sweeping stone steps of Treshillick House, the stillness of their embrace making them look like one of those biped photographs, with its grey image slightly creased and faded by time.

Now, though, I needed to turn to my own concerns, as the weather and the atmosphere were both changing rapidly, and instinct warned me to get on with establishing my own winter quarters, even while my body was already slowing down towards hibernation. I knew that I wouldn't cope with life above ground during an English winter, even in Cornwall's relatively mild climate, but the earth itself still waited beneath me, ready to embrace my cool-blooded body with its own encompassing warmth. And the Major had left me a good supply of hay to bed myself down comfortably, and straw to cover and protect myself.

With the Major having gone away and winter approaching, a state of torpor seemed to settle over the whole of Treshillick, like the stillness of winter itself. For myself, nature had already dealt with the small, nourishing meals I'd eaten during the early autumn, and had then cooled both appetite and activity until my metabolism was ready for hibernation. My *hibernaculum* was ready, underneath the sheltering hedge: all I had to do now, as the irresistible and welcoming sleepiness began to engulf me, was to settle myself comfortably in my bed of hay, pulling the straw and the leaves down on top of me. I think Rosie must have helped a little with that task: I sensed small hands patting my protective coverings snugly into place around me, while her soft voice floated down from far above, lulling my senses as I drifted away into that fathomless, earthy deep which is natural to my kind.

Birdsong, high and insistent, reached down to call me towards the surface as I was beginning to rouse and stir within the softness of my bed. Along with the first hint of returning warmth just starting to permeate the earth, the effect on my senses was compelling.

Instinct told me it was time to move, but it would take many days for me to surface completely, in this unpredictable northern climate. Back in the Mediterranean, I would simply throw off my covering of warm, sandy soil to emerge into a sunlight which was already strong and reviving. Here, by contrast, I spent the first few days gradually sticking my neck out a short way, sniffing the air, and then retreating into my dugout to drowse again.

But the call of the new season is as insistent in England as it is in Greece: it just takes longer for a solar-powered creature like me to respond. In those days of natural hibernation, rather than the later, biped-assisted fridge-to-*vivarium* version, I would unbury myself very slowly, taking my time until the sun could do its work. Then I would make my slightly unsteady way out from beneath the hedge, but still protected by its bulk as I dozed in the spring sunshine. Appetite would gradually return, when I would start by making tentative inroads into the nearest grass and new dandelion leaves.

By the time the winds eased and the balmy Cornish spring days arrived, I could venture further afield in my field, and it was on one of these days that Rosie first came to find me once more. Her delight at seeing me was evident, as was mine when she produced from her pocket some early salad leaves, which I accepted readily. Piling up my discarded straw for a seat, Rosie settled herself against the hedge to watch me eating. When I'd finished the salad, she carefully used a pocket knife to cut small pieces from the apple she'd been holding rather triumphantly. Those apple pieces seemed to me then the sweetest morsels I'd ever eaten; refreshing, reviving and rehydrating, all at once.

Meanwhile, my other female companion, the one belonging to my own species, had also emerged from hibernation and now required her share of my attention. This time, there was no need to fight for the right to mate, as there had been for Shelley's memorably poetic lines back in Greece. But this female in Cornwall had a certain Greek-style classical grace of her own. In fact, given my strong instinct to mate, she appeared to me to possess all The Three Graces at once, in that she embodied charm in her own readiness to mate, creativity in her very being, and beauty in simply being a female of my own species, here in these English fields. So I called her Gracie Fields, and sang my mating song.

In due course, then, Gracie ambled off, just as Shelley had done. I didn't see her again: I think the Major had left instructions that she should have a pasture of her own, to let her nest and feed undisturbed. Sadly, though, instinct must have warned Gracie, as it warned me, that we were unlikely to succeed in our efforts at chelonian colonization, so far north: even Cornwall's mildness is too cool for tortoise eggs to produce hatchlings outdoors. But we did try.

Rosie's regular visits continued to be an important and enjoyable part of the pattern of my spring days. In fact, I began to hope that we could continue like this and spend another idyllic summer in the meadow, just as we'd done the previous year.

I suppose the letter, when it arrived one morning as the summer was approaching its solstice, was the juvenile equivalent of the adult bipeds' call-up papers, except that this was more of a call-down paper. Rosie settled herself on the grass beside me, and read it out in a very small voice. I couldn't really understand much of it, myself, but I began to realise from the way Rosie spoke that she and Bob would be going home, back to the bipeds' war-damaged city.

"I feel so strange, Jerry. *'Course* I want to go home, see Mum, and maybe Dad'll be back from the war, too. But I've sort of got used to living in Cornwall, and so's Bob. I like the tiny little school, and Treshillick's lovely big kitchen – and your field, Jerry."

She came to say goodbye to me one warm, sunny morning. I was basking alongside the old wall, when her shadow fell across me. Crouching down beside me, as she'd done so often before, she picked me up gently and held me to her. As she lowered her face towards me to whisper her farewells, I felt drops of moisture on my shell, which were falling from her eyes.

"I'll come back and see you one day, Jerry – I promise."

I felt myself being propped gently against the wall once again; and then Rosie was gone.

Chapter 8: Pasture-ized
Immersed in the Jerry-can spirit

The bipeds' war was over. But there had been no immediate celebration at Treshillick: far from it, in fact, particularly after Rosie had said her sad goodbye. Now that she and Bob had gone, and with no sign of the Major's return from the war just yet, the place felt rather empty, that midsummer.

The Cornish bipeds carried on with their rural traditions, though, and even reinstated some of their pre-war celebrations, which included the rather alarming practice of lighting hilltop bonfires all across Cornwall on the night before the summer solstice. That sort of thing is fine for the bipeds, of course – each species is entitled to its own tastes, naturally – but it can be very disconcerting for everyone else, when bipeds go around lighting fires all over the place. Generally, we in the animal kingdom deplore the bipeds' habit of messing about with fire at the least opportunity, particularly in areas which they share with the rest of us, since fire tends to lead to all sorts of problems. This is often the case when the bipeds are over-excited or become careless. On this annual occasion, though, which the Cornish bipeds call St John's Eve as their version of Midsummer's Eve, I have to admit that everything was always very well organised at Treshillick, with the fire kept confined and strictly under control.

The scent of woodsmoke reached me just as I was settling down for the night under my hedge, so I stuck my neck out just to make absolutely sure that there was no danger threatening. There wasn't: the fire had been lit safely in a gently sloping field on the other side of the stream, where the bipeds seemed to be enjoying themselves hugely, singing and dancing by the firelight and the moonlight, and eating and drinking as I hadn't seen them do before. I was glad for them; after all, they'd suffered terribly in their recent war, as I knew only too well. But I was happy to leave them to it, and retreat into my own, more peaceful world.

Midsummer turned out to be a particularly busy and noisy time amongst the Cornish bipeds. They very soon had another festival at Treshillick, this one being held exclusively for the Cornish bipeds to celebrate their way of life, their countryside, their traditions and Cornwall's subtle differences from the rest of the country. This Golowan Festival also involved singing, dancing and general merry-making in the field beyond the stream. Evidently the Cornish bipeds are very fond of their festivals, but their next celebration, towards the end of the summer, came much closer to home as far as I was concerned.

Preparations began while the weather was still hot (for England, anyway: in Greece I would have considered it just slightly warm), and the crops in my meadow were at their most bountiful. In the field beyond the stream, seating had been arranged in a large circle around a raised platform, on which various musical instruments were placed, with the usual tables laden with food and drink set out alongside. A procession of bipeds appeared, all dressed alike in blue robes with hoods, some carrying shield-shaped banners, so that they looked almost like a sky-coloured version of the ancient Romans' *testudo* formation. But these bipeds didn't appear to have any enemies to fight, on this occasion at least: the blue-robed bipeds settled themselves on the seating, while others gathered around them, beyond the circle. There seemed to be a lot more talking than usual, on this occasion, which was followed by singing and playing of the musical instruments, before the general feasting and merry-making. Having watched this spectacle for a while, I was on the point of losing interest and settling down for a snooze, when one of the bipeds left the gathering at the tables and began to walk purposefully down the field.

I watched this biped's progress. As he strode towards the stream I could see that he wasn't one of the blue-clad variety; as he splashed through the water I could see that he wore khaki; as he paused in the meadow with his eyes scanning the ground, I could finally see who he was.

We tortoises are notoriously slow and steady, but I put on a spurt of speed – relatively speaking – as soon as I recognised the Major. We met not far from my basking place against the old wall, he having covered rather more ground than I'd managed to do, even at my best speed. The next moment I found myself being lifted aloft and then being carried, face to face with my biped friend, till we came to rest at that favourite spot of ours beneath the oak tree.

And now, for me, the bipeds' war was truly over at last. My share in the world's upheaval had begun in my native North Africa and taken me across an entire continent, to fetch up in a Cornish meadow at the tip of England. For the Major, it had taken him in the opposite direction and subjected him to horrors which would stay with him, occasionally glimpsed behind his weary eyes, for the rest of his life.

But the Major's sole aim now, as he told me whilst sitting against the trunk of the tree, was to manage Treshillick to make it successful in this changing world. Even that festival, still going on in the field beyond the stream, was a part of the changes he had in mind: Gorsedh has long been an important event in Cornwall, with the blue-clad bipeds being Cornish Bards, which apparently means they know a lot about Cornwall and even speak its ancient language. I was glad to find that the Major had no intention of becoming a Cornish Bard, but had simply offered to host the festival because he felt it would be good for Treshillick to become more well-known in Cornwall generally.

The memoirs of Timothy – the tortoise who lived in Hampshire with the naturalist Gilbert White – were called *Notes of an English Country Tortoise* when Timothy's biped amanuensis had written it all down and turned it into a book. There in my meadow in Cornwall, I began to feel much as Timothy must have done in his garden in Hampshire, observing biped behaviour as life at Treshillick absorbed changes, though these were only subtle at first.

More of the Treshillick estate had been given over to farming during the war, and this process now intensified, as the bipeds needed to produce even more food. The Indian Stars had gone off to live in a tortoise sanctuary in Devon, on the other side of the river from Cornwall, since their pastures at Treshillick were needed for the bipeds' food production. But the Major assured me that their new meadow would be more suitable for their lifestyle, as it would include the latest advance in chelonian care: an artificially-heated indoor basking area. That sounded very impressive at the time, though it turned out to have been only a forerunner of my own, much later and more advanced *vivarium*. I hoped the Indian Stars would be content, but personally I had no desire to move on again, so I was very relieved to find out that my own pasture would be left untouched, as it was unsuitable for biped crops. In any case, the Major had other plans.

Those midsummer festivals had been only the start. The Major was convinced that Treshillick would have to change, if it wanted to survive, and I began to understand that the natural rules of evolution apply just as much to a Cornish estate as to an individual species in the animal kingdom. The next festival, at the time of the autumn equinox, celebrated the harvest of the bipeds' crops. This time, though, it was to be held in my own field. The Major very courteously came to see me about it beforehand, and assured me that as it would only take place in the evening, it wouldn't interfere with my own routine. I was perfectly content with this prospect of observing the bipeds at such close quarters, though still at a safe distance as I could watch from beneath my hedge. It would be a very interesting study, since by now I was becoming a serious student of biped habits.

The usual tables for food and drink were set out at one side of the field, and then the bipeds from the estate and the village all arrived while the late sun was still providing pleasant warmth. I recognised

George, the wartime friend of Rosie's brother Bob. He looked bigger now, as he brought his mother across the field to the hedge, and searched for me:

"There, Mum! They'm other tortoises went away, but this 'un, he's one of us, now – our Jerry, an' this field really belongs to him."

I felt very flattered at being considered such an integral part of Treshillick, so I tried to look as dignified as possible, rather like Jonathan posing nobly outside the Governor's residence in far-off St Helena. Other juvenile bipeds came to visit me, too, bringing tasty treats from the feast. The Major must have told them what sort of food I like: all except one little female, much smaller than my friend Rosie, who wanted to share her plateful with me. This consisted entirely of a helping of Guldize Pudding, which the Major told me afterwards is a Cornish speciality eaten at this particular festival. I didn't want to hurt this juvenile biped's feelings, of course, but the pudding wasn't at all to my taste. Admittedly it smelt of fruits, but evidently mixed with other biped foodstuffs which we chelonians definitely don't eat: flour and eggs, amongst other items which struck me as being even less savoury (so to speak), including animal fat. Fortunately, the Major must have realised what was happening. In his usual quiet, courteous way, he came to my rescue just at that moment, bearing slices of pear which he suggested that the small female should give me, instead of having to share her own helping of Guldize Pudding.

As usual on these occasions, the evening ended with dancing, and torches were lit in great metal baskets on tall poles. By now, all the local bipeds seemed to know that this was my field, so as they danced they cheerfully called out to each other:

"Mind Jerry!"

Or, laughingly:

"Not quite Gardy-Loo, but Gardy-Tort!"

When he came to see me the next day, the Major explained that 'Gardy-Loo!' was what the English bipeds in long-ago times used to shout when tipping waste water from the upper windows of their houses onto the street below, warning anyone who was passing to be careful. But this 'water' was actually their waste bodily fluids, the whole subject of which is a distinct peculiarity of biped behaviour. Anyway, the Major went on to decide that in Treshillick's case a call of 'Jerry-can!' would be more suitable, and then he laughed: the first time I'd heard him laugh since his return from the war.

I didn't know then, of course, that 'Jerry-can!' would become a sort of rallying-cry, which would follow me down the years and through all my subsequent dealings with the bipeds. It eventually extended as far as my own construction of that irrigation system for my crops in a Hampshire garden, which my biped family proudly referred to as the Jerry Can.

Meanwhile, though, during my time at Treshillick, I became fully immersed in the annual rituals of the estate, and perhaps just as importantly, in the spirit of the place: a spirit of peace and the appreciation of relative bounty. The seasons revolved; I dug a fresh *hibernaculum*; the following summer passed as pleasantly as the previous one had done. Now, though, there was a steady increase in biped activity in and around my field, as more of those festivals and events were held.

The next winter was an exceptionally snowy one, right across Great Britain. Even Cornwall lay under a thick covering of snow. Of course, I was safely underground before the snow fell, my bodily systems already inured to the cold. But I could tell, on rousing rather later than usual in the following, reluctant springtime, that the cold had been severe. The earth was unyielding, and all creatures were late in stirring. Even the birds were not yet busy. While I was still on my way to the surface and dozing peacefully in my hay bed, the Major arrived carrying a large box, and lifted me gently to place me inside. Too sleepy to concern myself with whether this might be yet another travelling-box, I simply snuggled down into the fresh hay and drowsed again.

Once the winter had finally released its grip and I was fully awake, my first idea was that I might be back in the hold of that military transport ship. But beneath this box there was no lurching, sickening movement, and as I moved to peer cautiously over the side, I realised I was in some sort of wood-planked shelter which smelt of livestock. The air remained chill, so I was glad of this early form of *vivarium*. The Major came every day to check on me and, as the temperature rose and my desire for activity increased, he began to hand-feed me the necessary juicy snacks, by way of encouraging me to break my fast. And then I was out in my field once more, foraging, checking on my crops and generally taking my allotted part in the life of Treshillick.

Although I missed my first and best young friend, Rosie, I still had plenty of biped company, with the Major's visits and an increasing number of juvenile bipeds coming to Treshillick for nature study lessons and for games, throughout the summer. They would always seek me out in my field, and courteously invite me to join in their picnics, which would be spread out on the grass under the oak tree. By the time they left, I would be full of such delights as lettuce, cucumber and strawberries, and in need of a restorative doze beside the old wall.

Summer evenings would sometimes bring groups of rather bigger young females, dressed all alike in blue. On the first occasion, I thought these must be juvenile Cornish Bards, although their blue garments weren't voluminous robes, but practical-looking straight dark blue from middle to knees, with lighter blue tops sporting brightly-coloured badges – rather like the insignia on the Major's khaki – and small, variously-coloured cloth strips fluttering from one shoulder. They each wore a smart-looking tie, too, with a badge glinting in the sunlight, while on their heads they wore dark blue hats instead of hoods. And anyway, they didn't do the same things as the Bards had done. They did carry a banner ceremonially into the field, though – modern bipeds seem to be just as fond of their banners as their ancestors were – but this part of their activities wasn't on the same scale as the Bards' ceremonies had been. All the blue-clad females stood to form a horseshoe shape around their banner, accompanied by two adult females similarly dressed, who were clearly in charge. They held some sort of ceremony, involving talking which by now I could hear was in English not Cornish, so that told me they definitely weren't Bards.

After the ceremony, which was much shorter than the Bards' version had been, these juveniles formed smaller groups, each led by one of the biggest members who would call her group together by blowing a shrill blast on the whistle attached to her clothing by a white cord, and each group then busied itself with its allotted task. One group went down to the stream, to study the wildlife there; another set off for the nearest belt of woodland, to lay tracks for a different group to follow; yet another settled down beneath the oak tree in the middle of the field, to practise bandaging each other's limbs and making stretchers to carry incapacitated bipeds. Then they all played games, involving a lot of running around while laughing and calling to each other.

Meanwhile, the adults had been busy unpacking provisions, and a few of the juveniles emerged from the woods carrying sticks and dried leaves. Next, they cut away a square of turf and began to arrange the leaves and sticks on the hard earth beneath. Of course, all these preparations could mean only one thing: the usual biped obsession with fire. I retreated in good order to my hedgerow, from where I could keep an eye on the proceedings and make sure things didn't get out of hand.

Once the fire was alight, the whole group gathered together again, this time around their admittedly well-tended fire. Some sort of light meal was cooked, with evident concentration, by holding out the items of food over the fire on long, green sticks, which had been prepared by peeling away the bark. I was relieved to see that these bipeds understood and respected fire, and even knew which sticks to use: hazel and ash are safe enough, but birch is poisonous, and I certainly didn't want a lot of poisoned bipeds lying about all over my field. But these young female bipeds seemed to be in the peak of condition, as they chatted and laughed. After their meal the whole group sang songs together, their enjoyment showing clearly on their faces. Finally, as dusk was deepening, the fire was put out, the square of turf replaced and watered, and the field tidied, before the bipeds and their equipment melted away into the gathering darkness.

I'd thoroughly enjoyed my evening's study of these biped activities. The next day, the Major explained it all to me, saying that as everyone had been so well-behaved and left my field so tidy, he'd invited the whole group to come again. Apparently these females were – and still are, nowadays – called Girl Guides, who are organised in companies not just across Cornwall, but all over Great Britain and beyond. The significance of that hadn't escaped me, but the seasons of the year would revolve more than once, before my hope about the Girl Guides would become reality.

Chapter 9: Guided tour
Days of mine and Rosie's

The Major must have organised it, though I think he enjoyed leaving me to unearth this particular treat for myself.

A different company of Girl Guides had arrived one summer's afternoon. Although they looked generally the same as the local Guides, in their blue uniform, I knew they were different because their ties weren't the same colour as the ones worn by the Treshillick Guides. But the same little gold badge still glinted on each Guide's tie. Anyway, this company set about unpacking mounds of equipment, far more than one evening's-worth; these Guides must be staying. Sure enough, I watched as tents, smaller than the military ones I'd seen back in North Africa, were put up around the field, and armfuls of bedding were then carried inside. A bigger tent was clearly to be used for stores, as several pairs of Guides staggered inside, bearing between them boxfuls of provisions.

Meanwhile, further down my field towards the stream, other preparations were going on. These were of a type which was familiar enough to me by now, so the generally increased level of activity didn't really bother me, even though it involved the usual biped fascination with fire. Several Guides emerged from the woods bringing large quantities of sticks tied in bundles, having left the smaller members of their group to rummage for dried leaves under my hedgerow. I didn't begrudge these fellow-foragers the few handfuls of leaves they took, as there were always plenty lying around; more than enough for my own needs. Another group was busy in an open part of the field, cutting out a piece of turf and building a fireplace, which was on a larger scale than the local Guides usually made during their evening visits. A substantial woodpile gradually grew up nearby, with the sticks being carefully sorted and arranged according to size. Intending to retire as usual beneath my hedgerow and observe the proceedings from there, I set off purposefully from my basking place.

It was then that she found me. She emerged from rummaging particularly thoroughly under the hedge; the smallest Guide of them all, dressed in blue just like the others but, to me, definitely not just like the others. She started up as I approached, and dropped her cargo of leaves with a cry:

"*Jerry!* There you are – I knew I'd find you!"

And then, laughing, Rosie picked me up, as gently as always. Sitting against the hedge with me on her lap, she told me all about joining the Guides, and how she'd written to tell the Major, with the result that he'd invited the whole company to camp at Treshillick. While she was still chattering to me excitedly, one of the bigger Guides came over:

"So *there* you are, Rosie – and this must be Jerry, the evacuee friend you've told us so much about! Well, why don't you bring him over to meet Captain and the others?"

Rosie and I made our way across the field – she carrying me carefully, and I enjoying a biped's-eye view of my domain – to where some more Guides were busy making their ceremonial place, energetically banging pegs into the ground for strong ropes to secure a tall pole for their banner.

Proudly, but rather shyly, Rosie introduced me to one of the adult females, who stroked my shell and gravely said how pleased she was to meet me. Then she turned to Rosie once more.

"And now, Rosie, you'd better settle Jerry back underneath his hedge, well out of harm's way while we finish pitching camp. But perhaps you'd like him to join us for campfire this evening? Mind, though: you'll have to take *very* great care of him, and keep him well away from the fire. In fact, Jerry can be your special responsibility for the whole time we're camping here. It'll all count towards the Friend to Animals badge that you're so keen to work for."

Rosie was delighted, stammering out her thanks and her promise to look after me. Personally, I was a little nervous of being anywhere near a fire, but I soon decided that if an adult biped – the Guide Captain, at that – could trust Rosie, then so could I. Besides, the Captain had unintentionally used that phrase which had already become my own guiding motto: *Jerry can.* So, if Rosie was going to work for some kind of recognition as a friend to animals, then of course I would do everything I could to help her. As far as I was concerned she'd already proved herself, many times over, during our shared experience of taking refuge from the bipeds' world war.

On our way back to my hedge, Rosie and I passed yet more Guides, who were putting up small shelters in an unused corner of the field, ready for something which Rosie called latrines. During the time that the Guides spent sharing my field, it became apparent – since we tortoises have a very keen sense of smell –

that these were, in fact, a much less unpleasant version of those Gardy-Loos which the Major had told me about. In this case, though, I rather think they must have been called Guidey-Loos.

That first evening's campfire was only a small one, according to Rosie, but it seemed huge to me, as I kept an eye on the leaping flames, listened to the crackle of the logs and smelt the woodsmoke, all from the safety of Rosie's lap. But as it turned out, my favourite part of the Guides' day soon became the evening, when dusk was falling and these high-spirited but peaceable bipeds would gather around their fire, discussing the day's activities, making plans for the next day, and always including me whenever they could. Rosie and I invariably settled ourselves well back from the fire itself, of course, giving me an excellent overall view of the proceedings.

A large can of water was suspended from a tripod made out of sturdy sticks, to hang above the flames. While this can was heating, the Guides carefully held out their pieces of food on long sticks to toast near the fire, just as the local Guide company liked to do. Rosie was much too concerned for my safety to join in with this part of the evening's entertainment, so one of the bigger Guides would bring hot titbits to her, on a tin plate which would be set down at Rosie's side. While most of the Guides were squealing and laughing over the hot food, the biggest ones helped the adults to make hot drinks using water from the steaming can, which they first placed on the ground and then carefully tilted into tin mugs, levering the can with a large forked stick. Of course Rosie's comment, whispered to me that first evening, was:

"Oh, look – it's a Jerry can!"

As the daylight faded and the firelight intensified, the Guides sang songs, while their faces seemed to glow: Rosie's most of all, naturally. Eventually I withdrew into my shell and settled down to doze on her lap, rousing only slightly when the fire had burned low and Rosie carried me carefully to my bed of leaves under the hedgerow.

The Guides' daytime activities proved to be just as interesting for me to study, though I didn't take such an active role in these, myself. I preferred to hear about them afterwards from Rosie, since all that biped-style dashing about can be rather tiring, particularly where groups of very active juveniles are concerned.

Their day started early – in biped terms, that is, since I was always up before they had even stirred, this being high summer. By the time the first juvenile bipeds emerged from their tents, yawning, I would already be sunning myself just beyond the hedgerow, and thinking of stopping off to do a little foraging on my way to the old wall. But with Rosie around, I didn't need to bother, as she would come padding across the grass to find me. Still in her striped pyjamas and with bare feet, she had stopped only long enough to pick some tender clover and juicy dandelions for my breakfast. While I munched my way through these, Rosie would squat down beside me in the grass – already drying in the early morning sun – and tell me of the Guides' plans for the day, before running back across the field and disappearing into one of the wash-tents.

Once they were all washed and dressed, and the usual can of water had been set to heat above the fire, the bipeds held a short ceremony beside their banner, before gathering for their breakfast at the long tables set up outside the stores tent. I was pleased to see that they ate heartily, before they dispersed in their smaller groups for their allotted jobs: washing plates and mugs in bowls of steaming water, gathering more wood to replenish the pile, and going to fetch further supplies of food from Treshillick House. Rosie called these smaller groups 'patrols', and proudly showed me the badge she wore with a picture of a bird on it, to show which patrol she belonged to: her badge showed a soaring skylark. The coloured strips fluttering from one shoulder of each Guide's uniform were the colours of the different patrols, too: brown and grey for the Skylark Patrol, brown and red for the Robin Patrol, brown and gold for the Tortoise Patrol... At least, that would have been the case if reptiles had been allowed as well as birds, of course. Rosie and I both felt this would be perfectly appropriate, and anyway, I rather liked the idea of her wearing the emblem of her very own heraldic tortoise on her uniform.

After the Guides' various jobs were finished, Rosie would come over to see me again before they all set off on whatever expedition they had planned for that morning. I would set off, too, for my basking place beside the old wall. There I could settle down peacefully, content in the knowledge that Rosie was back here in Cornwall once more, just as she'd promised, and was enjoying herself.

Midday was heralded by an equally cheerful bustle, as the bipeds returned to camp and set about making their main meal of the day. This always included vegetables or salad of some sort, and ended with summer fruits, so it became a very pleasant highlight of my own day, too, since Rosie was as determined as ever that I shouldn't be left out. In fact, I looked forward to this part of the day almost as much as to the evening's campfire.

After the meal came another part of the Guides' routine which suited me very well: 'rest hour', when the juvenile bipeds would disappear into their tents to doze or read, or sit chatting quietly in the dappled shade outside. This was when Rosie and I would settle ourselves on the groundsheet spread outside her patrol's tent. Softly, she would tell me of that morning's adventures, and show me the treasures she'd gleaned. These might be wild flowers, which she pressed carefully between the pages of a book (I was pleased to see that she still carried books with her), or a discarded bird's feather, or seashells after a hike to the beach.

One of the most memorable of these excursions, from my own point of view, was the day when the Guides had visited an old Cornish tin mine. This reached deep underground – much deeper than I would ever dream of digging for hibernation purposes – and during that day's rest hour, Rosie showed me the small pieces of rock she'd collected. They didn't look much to me; on the contrary, it struck me that they would have made for very arduous digging, but

Rosie was enchanted, and stowed them away carefully with her other souvenirs.

Apparently the Cornish miners were so adept at working underground that some of them decided to go mining much further afield. According to Rosie, there's even a saying amongst the bipeds that if you look in any hole in the ground, anywhere in the world, you'll find a Cornish biped at the bottom, searching for metal. I've never found one myself, but naturally I didn't doubt the truth of Rosie's information, so it had to be that I've simply never needed to dig down that far. I decided this was probably for the best, as I couldn't imagine settling down for a peaceful winter's sleep with an adjacent biped bashing away at rocks all around my *hibernaculum*.

While she was at the mine, Rosie had also learned that the Cornish banner, with its white cross on a black background, was viewed by the miners as representing the lighter Cornish tin making lines through the dark rocks. That's fine as far as it goes, of course, but it convinced me even further that the Cornish banner would be greatly improved – at least in its mine-boring aspect – if it bore (as it were) the figure of a heraldic tortoise; not rampant on this occasion, perhaps, but dormant, as if deep in hibernation.

After their rest hour, the Guides would go on another expedition, though much shorter than the morning's trip. They usually took a picnic tea – after inviting me to sample the tastiest ingredients – and set off for the cliffs beyond Treshillick's grounds, or for the shortcut down to the beach. At that point, I would have my own rest hour, making my way to the old wall to settle down and doze gently, while musing on everything that Rosie had told me so far that day. Naturally I enjoyed the peaceful sensation of having my field to myself again for a while, after so much activity, but that didn't stop me looking forward with real pleasure to the prospect of another evening with my biped companions.

Their final evening came at last, of course. That night's campfire was an extra special one, with more food and more songs than on previous evenings, and with several of the Guides standing up to recite or sing alone. This was mostly done by the bigger ones, so I was surprised when Rosie stood up – still holding me carefully – and asked to recite a story. I was even more surprised to find that it was a story I knew instinctively, from my own juvenile days back in North Africa. There in the firelight, holding me to her so that all eyes were on us both, Rosie told the story of *The Tortoise and the Hare*. I felt enormously proud of her.

This time, when she came to say goodbye to me, there were no drops of water falling from Rosie's eyes. There was only a slight wistfulness in her voice, as she promised to return next year. By then, I knew her well enough not to doubt her word for that.

Rosie certainly did keep her promise to visit me again. In fact, she came each summer for several years, always with the Guides, and always just as eager to spend as much time with me as possible. Those Guide camps became a particular highlight, not simply of my summer, but of my whole year. In addition to all my everyday concerns in my own domain, and my continuing interaction with the Major and other Cornish bipeds, I relished these opportunities to check on the progress of my special, juvenile biped friend. From her being the smallest in the camp that first summer, I watched Rosie grow, and develop in confidence and understanding as she matured.

The next summer, she could hardly wait to find me and to tell me all about her Friend to Animals badge, which she wore proudly displayed on the sleeve of her uniform. Apparently she'd been allowed to keep a rabbit at home – presumably the nearest animal to a hare that she could get – and had been busy finding out about various other animals, too, and the best ways for bipeds to care for them. Again, I was proud of her. By the summer after that, Rosie was definitely one of the bigger Guides, and helping the smaller ones to learn the ropes – literally, as I watched her showing them how to secure ropes for the tents and for the inevitable banner.

Eventually, there came the summer when Rosie was practically the biggest juvenile in the camp. By now she was leading her own patrol, and would introduce the younger juveniles to me and my way of life, with a cheerful authority which belied her own still-juvenile status. Privately, in those quiet rest hour moments which she and I still cherished, Rosie told me of her plans for the future. She would soon be too old for the Guides, so she would move on to something called the Rangers, although she wasn't at all sure that she could persuade them to come and camp at Treshillick.

Rosie's life would change in other ways, too, as she was starting to think about what she wanted to do as an adult. I'd expected her to decide she wanted to look after animals, but apparently it would take a very long time to learn – since we in the animal kingdom are highly complex creatures – and anyway, at that time there were still very few female bipeds treating sick animals. Rosie's caring nature wasn't limited to animals, though: it extended to bipeds, too, and she'd decided to become a nurse, looking after juvenile bipeds in particular. I approved, of course, as I knew that type of occupation would suit her character. After all, I'd seen her dealing with the younger Guides, competently taking care firstly, perhaps, of one who'd fallen over and grazed her knee, then reassuring another who might be feeling rather overwhelmed by her very first camping expedition.

I nudged Rosie's enveloping arm gently with my head, just to make sure she knew I approved. She did: we understood each other perfectly, and we both knew that somehow, whatever happened, Rosie would make her eventual way back to Cornwall.

This time, though, it would be far longer until that particular promise could be fulfilled. But at least neither of us had any idea of exactly how long, as Rosie said goodbye to me at the end of that final summer camp, leaving me to settle once more into my peaceful routine at Treshillick.

Chapter 10: A sad estate of affairs
The new battle for survival

Naturally I hadn't been ignoring the Major during Rosie's summertime visits. He was still my main source of both companionship and information, as he continued his regular checks on my field, my hedgerow and my general well-being. As always, we would settle down together beneath the old oak tree or beside the hedge.

It was during these quiet, companionable times that I began to realise the extent of the problems faced by Treshillick, in common with other rural estates in Cornwall and beyond. The recent war among the bipeds had changed not only their view of the wider world, but even the way they ran their own local affairs. The warring factions had been busily killing each other to such an extent that there weren't enough of them left to run their farms, or to produce all the other things which bipeds seem to need in order to survive. Their food was still in short supply and shared out very strictly. The Major explained this as 'rationing', which worried me at first, until I found that dandelions, clover and even the wild strawberries in my field weren't included in rationing. Anyway, it seemed that rationing only had to be applied to bipeds and not to anyone else, which was quite right, when you come to think about it, since it had been the bipeds' war, with the animal kingdom in general only being caught up in it as innocent bystanders.

After the war Treshillick continued to produce as much food as possible, for its biped and animal populations alike, but now there simply weren't enough bipeds on the estate to do all the necessary work. So the Major seemed to be taking on more and more of the tasks himself, in the absence of helpers such as the father of George, the Cornish juvenile who had played in my field with our evacuee friends Rosie and Bob. George's father had never come home from the war. But by this time George, like Rosie, was approaching adulthood himself, and was doing his best to take his father's place.

Now, though, whenever the Major came to see me, there was no more reading from a book pulled from his pocket, to while the time away pleasantly as the shadows lengthened. Looking tired and even a little dishevelled, he would simply flop down against the oak tree and stroke my shell with a weary sigh:

"Oh, Jerry. This is all getting a bit trying. George is a good lad – he's taking on as much as he can, and probably more than he should. But the farm simply can't support the whole estate for much longer; I've just got to come up with other ways to increase our income."

I didn't really understand the problem of income, myself, since it's another purely biped concept which doesn't apply to the rest of us. But I did recognise the Major's sense of heavy responsibility for the bipeds on the estate, such as George and his mother. I could only show my sympathy for the Major's plight by nudging his hand gently with my head. He seemed to appreciate my gesture of support.

But biped affairs do have an effect on the rest of us, of course, even if we don't entirely understand them. After all, Treshillick had become my home, and I certainly didn't want that situation to alter. Neither did the Major, for himself or for any of us who were left, so the pace of change on the estate itself began to increase, in an effort to secure the future for all of us.

The first noticeable difference, as far as I was concerned personally, was in the part of Treshillick's grounds nearest to my own domain. After the success of the Guides' camping expeditions – which the Major had offered to them without any benefit to the estate other than their presence, really for Rosie's sake – he decided to offer it to the male bipeds' version. These 'Scouts' would be coming from all over Cornwall, so their camping place would need to be much larger; not in my meadow, but in the big field beyond the stream. More importantly for the estate, it would mean the Scouts giving something back to Treshillick in return for being allowed to camp. This would apparently help the Major with the income he needed, while these strong young male bipeds were also very happy to help out on the farm, in between their own excursions. I understood the various camping activities quite well, of course, after Rosie's explanations during the Guides' visits, so this time I simply settled down to watch from my hedgerow. Without Rosie to look out for me, it seemed the only safe plan – particularly when these enthusiastic juveniles started handling dangerous-looking farm implements, splashing through the stream and hauling loaded carts across my field.

The Major was clearly very pleased with this first venture, so the success of the Scouts' visit encouraged him to expand the estate's activities to include even more biped events. That autumn, as he checked on my preparations for hibernation, the

Major proudly told me of his female's plans to hold a midwinter fair in Treshillick House itself, inviting local craftsmen to display their wares, which other bipeds would want to come and see, and exchange for income. All this activity meant that I was beginning to understand how the bipeds' system of income worked. As I got busy digging that year's *hibernaculum*, I was very glad to leave the bipeds to their own devices, but I hoped the winter would prove successful for them.

It did: in fact, the Major seemed very pleased, when he told me all about it the following spring. Now his plans gathered pace, with more events and fairs to be held inside the house, and even more bipeds milling about outside it, too. In addition to the summer fair to be held on the lawn in front of the house, parts of the grounds would be opened to the biped population at large, while the rose garden would be open for visitors during its midsummer flowering season.

But I was relieved to learn that I wouldn't be disturbed by this event: the local Guides, who were going to steer the visiting bipeds around the garden as far as the old wall, proceeded to tie a stout rope across the archway between the rose garden and my field. Not content with the Guides' precautions, though, George had decided to guard my side of the archway himself, at the busiest times. He would take the opportunity to sit in the grass alongside me and put one of those small white sticks in his mouth, which bipeds like to set alight to produce smoke and a rather peculiar smell. I'll never understand the bipeds' fascination with fire.

Anyway, sitting beside me, George began to talk about his concerns for the Major and the estate:

"Major needs me, Jerry: he'm not so young as he were, then there's Dad gone an' all. Major reckons I can help with running this place, now, 'specially as I won't be going for National Service, me being in farming."

That sounded fine, as far as I understood it: George had grown up on the estate and probably knew it almost as well as the Major himself, who had no juveniles of his own. So I basked peacefully in George's easy company, while remaining aware – through the warm, soft earth – of everything that was happening on the other side of the wall, content that so many bipeds had come to enjoy the rose garden.

That summer set the pattern for all the summers that followed, throughout the years I lived at Treshillick. The summer after the rose garden's first opening was when the bipeds' food rationing had finally come to an end, so Treshillick celebrated by offering afternoon tea to visitors (English bipeds are very fond of their afternoon tea), which would need to be served in my field. Here the visitors could view the rose garden, the stream and the estate's woods and fields. The Major came to see me about the arrangements, of course; I was perfectly happy to host this event, and even happier to help with the clearing up afterwards, as English afternoon tea in the garden invariably involves plenty of luscious strawberries…

Meanwhile the Major's female, along with George's mother and her helpers, were all very busy preparing some of Treshillick's own produce for the visitors. A large tent was set up, rather like the

Guides' stores; platters of food were carried out, and tables were set out around the oak tree for the visitors. I knew from my experiences with Rosie that tea involves hot water, but I was pleased to see there were no preparations for a fire. Instead, George and another juvenile trundled a handcart towards the tent, bearing an enormous can which they called an urn. Watching proceedings from my hedgerow as usual, I was pleased to see the bipeds, after all the strains of their war, sitting in the warm afternoon sun to enjoy their beloved tea in the peaceful grounds of Treshillick.

As the years passed and the Major grew more confident in expanding the estate's activities, I gradually became accustomed to the different events going on around me. Sometimes, though, they still came as a surprise.

Take the first time I saw bipeds riding horses around a field, for instance. Horses, like all animals with hooves, are to be avoided as far as I'm concerned, for obvious reasons. But a horse plus a biped – particularly when the horse leaps over fences with the biped on its back – always strikes me as a particularly dangerous combination. Not that it ever did strike me, of course, since I was keeping well out of the way. This event was held each summer for several years, and involved a lot of small bipeds riding small horses. Not content with jumping over fences, they played horse-and-biped games, too. These involved complicated-looking races with the horses going round obstacles while their bipeds leant down to pick up objects such as small banners. These were then carried aloft by the bipeds, bouncing about as their horses raced towards a length of coloured ribbon where the adult bipeds stood cheering. This all took place in the field beyond the stream, and I was very glad to be watching from my usual safe distance.

Far less dangerous were the open-air plays, held each midsummer. These involved a group of robed bipeds on a raised platform, striding about and saying a lot of words very loudly, while more bipeds were seated in a semi-circle, so it all looked rather like the meetings of the Cornish Bards. The Major had decided to hold this annual event in my field, so that refreshments could be enjoyed in the adjacent rose garden. Courteous as ever, he came to explain it all to me beforehand, and told me the plays had been written down by a very famous Bard – though not of the Cornish variety – called Shakespeare. I didn't mind accommodating Shakespeare in my field, although the only play I remember was the one which, so the Major told me, was about a soldiering ancient Roman. I can still remember my disappointment on finding that the play didn't actually feature the Roman army's *testudo* protection, as I'd been particularly looking forward to that.

Generally, though, the most interesting feature of the plays, as far as I was concerned, was the apparent ability of these robed bipeds to change colour, unlike the blue-robed Cornish Bards. Some of them would leave the platform, and return later displaying some completely un-biped-like hues. I wondered at first whether these particular bipeds could somehow be related to my own distant cousins, the chameleons. But, to my disappointment, they'd only changed their robes and painted bright colours on their faces and bodies.

Though Treshillick had never actually been bombed during the bipeds' war – I'd seen quite enough of that, in North Africa and Greece – it now suffered something of a bombshell, as the Major called it. This was a slightly unfortunate description, in my view, but we chelonians don't actually shudder in the way that bipeds do. The problem for Treshillick was that George and his mother were going to leave, and travel to join relatives in a place called America. Apparently lots of English bipeds wanted to go to America after the war, but even somewhere as vast as America couldn't take them all, so they were only allowed to go if they had somewhere to live and work. George's relatives were offering him work on their own farm and a home there for himself and his mother.

It was about this time that the Major began to look increasingly tired and worried. Of course, I knew by instinct that bipeds age far more quickly than tortoises, but now my biped friend was ageing noticeably fast. He continued to soldier on throughout the next few years, determined to make the estate a success. And so my own peaceful routine was punctuated by the ever widening range of events in Treshillick's grounds.

The Shakespeare plays became a regular feature and proved very popular, judging by the crowds of bipeds who came. The summer fairs and open days became larger and more frequent, too, although the Major always came to see me first, whenever my field was needed, and made sure I was safe.

The horse-riding didn't turn out to be quite so popular, which was privately quite a relief to me, as I wasn't keen on having all those horses trampling about; far too dangerous. Within a few years, though, that event had been replaced by a 'motor show'. This involved a lot of rather noisy and smelly machines being brought onto the estate – thankfully nowhere near my own domain – for the bipeds to study and admire. The Major said these machines were cars, which happily weren't on the scale of the war machines I'd seen back in North Africa and in Greece, since cars didn't usually spew fire or make the earth tremble. This version of biped transport was much smaller, more like the cart on which I'd first arrived at Treshillick. Except that cars didn't need horses and seemed to work rather like the lawn mower I would witness much later, in my Hampshire family's garden. Anyway, the Major seemed pleased to have hosted his first motor show.

Another new venture for Treshillick was the annual music festival. By now, with George in America, the Major had taken on an estate manager to help him. This young manager appeared to have lots of new ideas, one of which was the music festival. I overheard him one spring morning, talking excitedly to the Major about it in the rose garden. It all sounded rather odd to me; this managing biped was hoping to arrange for a concert at Treshillick by The Beatles. I was rather startled at first, as I couldn't imagine why the bipeds would want to spend an evening listening to insect noises, until I realised from the Major's words that The Beatles weren't insects at all, but a group of music-making bipeds.

Next, the young manager thought he might try to get The Rolling Stones, but they couldn't come, either. This was a shame, as I'd been wondering whether they might be a local subspecies, perhaps sporting some sort of mobile carapace, and possibly even distantly related to the chelonian order. It would have been very interesting to meet some of my relations, but then I learned that The Rolling Stones, like The Beatles, were actually musical bipeds.

After all that, the music festival turned out to be a purely traditional biped affair, with music-making and singing by a group of bipeds on the raised platform, and more bipeds seated in front of them to listen. From my vantage point by the hedgerow, I found it all very soothing; I'm sure The Beatles' thrumming noises or The Rolling Stones' rocking noises wouldn't have had the same effect at all.

At the end of the concert, though, the soothing nature of the music was unceremoniously shattered – by fireworks. Instinct warns all animals to beware of fireworks: they whoosh, scream, and explode high in the sky in a multi-coloured blaze which then falls towards the earth like a fiery cloudburst. The noise can be terrifying, and strangely enough, some of the worst-affected animals are also some of the bipeds' best friends: dogs and horses. It's much easier for me, of course, as I simply retreat into my shell until it's all over. But the bipeds' love of fire is reflected in their love of fireworks, which they set off at every opportunity.

One of the last big events I remember at Treshillick, before my world changed completely yet again, was a sadder occasion: the Major decided to raise some income not for the estate itself, but for the families of some Cornish bipeds who'd recently been lost at sea. Apparently this was called the Penlee Lifeboat Disaster, when several bipeds from another part of Cornwall had put to sea in terrible midwinter weather conditions, trying to rescue some other bipeds whose ship had been hurled against rocks. They all died.

Having been at sea myself, I have at least a small idea of those bipeds' feelings of intense fear. But the crew of the Penlee Lifeboat didn't need to go to sea that night; they went out purely to try to save others, overcoming their own survival instinct. It's what the bipeds call 'courage', and it's one of the biped qualities I've learned to admire the most.

The Major told me about it the following spring, when he was planning an even bigger summer fair that year, raising income to help the Penlee families. It was a huge success, with so many bipeds coming to Treshillick that they seemed to be swarming across the grounds, what with the gardens, the teas, the entertainments and the evening concert. The Major was delighted at the amount of income which it raised, but by now he was looking old and grey. His experiences of the war, and his constant efforts to keep Treshillick going ever since, had worn him out. I was becoming steadily more concerned about his health.

Chapter 11: Turning turtle
In deep water

I've always felt that some form of hibernation could offer at least a slight improvement to the woefully short lifespan of the bipeds. I'm sure their health would benefit if they would allow themselves longer periods of rest, and fewer bouts of the frenetic activity which is a commonly observed characteristic of the species. I mention this with the authority which comes from both instinct and experience, since my own species has evolved, slowly and steadily, to become one of the longest-lived on earth.

The Guides' rest hour had been an encouraging example of the bipeds' ability to work out this particular truth about longevity for themselves, of course, but a daily rest hour was so obviously inadequate for their longer-term needs. As for the Major himself, even a lengthy spell of hibernation would be insufficient to restore his former vitality, by this stage of his life. He still came to see me in my field, but nowadays he walked with the aid of a stick, and had difficulty even in bending down to touch me. His days of sitting comfortably in the grass alongside me were clearly over.

But the next bombshell, when it came, wasn't the one I'd begun to expect. I learned of it when I emerged from hibernation, the year after the fair had been held at Treshillick for the Penlee families. The Major came to see me as usual, although he himself was definitely not as usual. His hands trembled slightly, and there were new creases on his face; deep lines like the creases on the well-worn covers of the books he used to read, when he sat with me on board ship or in my field.

Instinct warned me of what the Major was about to say, before he'd even started to speak; the natural communication of intense feeling can more readily be understood, in receptive silence, than any biped words. But he evidently felt the need to tell me about it anyway, just as he'd told me so much else during all those summers in the meadow: his female had died during the winter.

The Major had evidently cared for his dying mate with that heartfelt devotion which the bipeds can often show, and I knew him well enough to have expected no less from him. But now that his female was gone, he was trying to make sense of the world without her.

Each species has its own way of viewing the world, naturally, and I've noticed that bipeds generally seem to feel the need to mourn their dead over an extended period of time, and usually with some sort of monument. As though they could somehow make life everlasting. The rest of us, by contrast, can do no more than view death briefly and silently, since the all-consuming business of staying alive means that we must each accept emptiness – even the total emptiness at the loss of a mate – in the continuing practical demands of the present.

That consideration didn't prevent my feelings of concern for the Major, though, particularly as the strain of his mate's death was clearly hastening his own decline. His former worries persisted, too, and even increased: insufficient income, and insufficient help on the farm. But now he had no lifelong partner to share his concerns.

And to all this, an even more serious problem was stealthily adding itself. I was probably the first to realise, as I knew by instinct that something was fundamentally wrong with my biped friend, and I've always found that instinct is infallible. The Major's memory was starting to fade. He had begun to confuse the recent past with the distant past, so that his memories of the war were more real, and becoming more important to him, than the latest concerns on the estate. He would still come and talk to me, leaning against the trunk of the old oak now that he could no longer sit beneath it, but his thoughts were becoming disjointed.

So, when he told me that the estate would have to be sold and different bipeds would then be in charge, I wasn't sure whether the Major's statement was the truth, or simply a rather confused expression of his own deepest fears. Somehow he managed to steer the estate through that summer, but the next shock came during the following autumn. The first serious sign of change was when I realised that the Major hadn't brought me the usual supply of hay and straw to help with my winter bedding. Not that it mattered too much for my own comfort, because there were always plenty of dry leaves and grasses which I could gather for myself on my foraging expeditions, by making my way along the length of the hedgerow and beside the old wall. But the Major's assistance had always been a very welcome kindness.

It was on one of these foraging expeditions to the old wall that I happened to see the Major leaving

Treshillick. He was sitting in a chair on wheels, which was being hoisted into a large white vehicle, rather like one of the cars at Treshillick's motor show. Except that this vehicle was larger than a car and had a red symbol on the side. As a white-clad biped moved towards the vehicle's back doors, I caught a glimpse of the Major's face: he was staring straight ahead, in my direction, but his eyes were expressionless and apparently unseeing. Then the doors were closed and the vehicle moved off down Treshillick's drive.

There was nothing else for me to do except to go on as usual with my preparations for winter. But as I drifted into the peaceful oblivion of hibernation, I sensed that my biped friend had begun his own process of sinking into a far deeper oblivion.

I roused particularly slowly, into the next Cornish springtime. This felt very different from the usual Cornish springtime, though; my first sensation on surfacing was a conviction that I would never see the Major again. I was facing another form of emptiness, different from the loss of a mate, but still painfully acute. I knew I'd lost a friend with whom I'd formed a very unusual bond: that deep empathy between two disparate creatures who had once been in common distress.

But the business of living must be continued, regardless of feelings. My first need was to protect myself from the cool dampness of the Cornish spring weather, giving my bodily systems the chance to warm up enough to begin functioning fully. In previous years the Major had helped me, by providing fresh bedding and even a place to stay in a barn, until the springtime really got going. Now, though, I would have to face the vagaries of this northern climate alone. So I withdrew into my shell once more, and waited for the sun to do its work.

My next sensation, on rousing fully, was a consciousness of the utter stillness all around me. The birds were singing lustily enough, but no sounds carried across from the direction of the farm, the gardens, or the house itself. The only movement came from a few cautious rabbits further down the field, and a pair of robins hopping about near the hedgerow, pausing now and then in their nest-building activities to regard me quizzically, heads on one side and black eyes shining. Eventually the stillness began to oppress me, so after breaking my fast on the new season's dandelions and grass, I set out from the hedgerow to investigate.

Making my way towards the old wall, I became aware of the smell of newly-turned earth mixed with dust and rubble. I knew that smell: it had first assailed me in North Africa when the warring bipeds set off their explosions, and again when I reached Greece and encountered the destruction there. I made my steady way – fuelled in equal measure by nutritious dandelions and a sense of foreboding – to the stone archway in the wall dividing my field from the rose garden. From there I would be able to look down the gentle slope towards the house.

I blinked slowly and carefully (my eyesight was already beginning to deteriorate), and looked again. Treshillick House was gone. In its place were piles of rubble, so that the whole area looked like a wartime bombsite, and in the midst of it all stood one of the bipeds' towering machines on its crushing runners. But instead of a long arm sticking out in front like the war machines I'd seen in the Mediterranean, this one had a long arm sticking upwards into the air, from the end of which hung a huge, vicious-looking ball. I thought at first that the bipeds must have started another of their wars, this time reaching all the way to Cornwall; perhaps I'd missed the most dangerous episodes, having already taken cover in my own underground shelter. In that case, though, where were the rest of the war machines, the soldiering bipeds, and those fire-spewing flying monsters of the genus *Spitfire*?

No, this couldn't be another biped war, mainly because there seemed to be no bipeds; the place looked abandoned and utterly desolate. I turned back to the comforting familiarity of the hedgerow. There, at least, I could settle down to think matters through, since these were deep waters indeed.

I knew the Major wouldn't have left without making some sort of provision for me if he possibly could. So he must have been too ill to manage his affairs, which certainly seemed to be the case when he was taken away, unseeing, in the white vehicle. That in turn meant the Treshillick estate must have been sold, as the Major had warned me the previous year, and there must be a new set of bipeds in charge, who obviously didn't want Treshillick House itself. And that knowledge led me to wonder what plans these new bipeds might have for the gardens and grounds – including my own domain.

I soon found out. As the days grew warmer and the ground became drier, more machines arrived and the earth seemed to shudder, as it had done in the bipeds' battlefields. I retreated beneath the hedgerow until the machines stopped, when I realised with relief that the bipeds had gone away again. Cautiously, the wildlife of Treshillick emerged once more, to resume its varied business. Once again I made my way to the stone arch in the wall.

No trace of the house remained; in its place was an enormous hole in the ground, like a huge and ugly wound. Most of the gardens had been flattened, too, almost as far as the wall which edged what used to be the rose garden. I thought of Rosie's story about Cornish mining bipeds being found at the bottom of any large hole, but I had no desire to investigate this particular crater, and retreated warily to my own side of the wall. My best hope now was that the meadow itself would be safe.

It wasn't. When the bipeds' machines broke through the old wall in midsummer, I knew I must, as the Major would have said, take evasive action. I made my way along the hedgerow, then down to where a belt of trees bordered the meadow, just above the stream. Food and shelter in that quiet corner were adequate, so I passed the summer watching from my new vantage point as the machines made their relentless way through the meadow, overturning everything in their path. Retreating further into cover, I began preparations early for my *hibernaculum*, digging deeper than ever into the comforting earth.

In springtime I roused into a totally different landscape. Only the old oak tree still stood as a

124

reminder of where the peaceful meadow had been; now, bipeds were scurrying all over it like giant ants. They were building small, low houses in a group around the tree, with rubble-strewn pathways between. As the noisy, dust-filled summer wore on, it became clear that each house would have its own small garden. This was encouraging, as it reminded me of the gardens in Greece, where I'd foraged successfully on my way from the bipeds' port to the tortoise haven in the hills. Perhaps I could still make my home in this new Treshillick – remembering Charles Darwin's motto about responding to change – and meanwhile the dandelions and clover at the edge of the meadow, and the watercress at the edge of the stream, would sustain me.

But the bipeds weren't finished yet. Machines now began to cut down the trees which I'd thought were my protection. No use turning back towards the new houses; no possibility of crossing the stream; no choice but to head for the other side of the belt of trees, and seek sanctuary in whatever landscape I would find there. Keeping close to the bank of the stream, I set off in a straight line, leaving the noise of tearing tree trunks and soughing branches as far behind me as I could.

When I eventually emerged from the trees and passed easily under a fence, I found myself at the edge of a close-cropped field, where the noise of sheep hung in the air. Then I saw them; the adults absorbed in feeding, the juveniles gambolling in all directions. I couldn't go back into the threatened trees, or forward into the moving flock; all I could do was retreat into my shell, and wait. But I was close to the stream, and the sheep were now making their way down to drink...

The pain didn't register until some moments after I'd heard the noise of my shell cracking. I remained withdrawn, shocked and nauseated by the impact of a hoof striking a glancing blow above one of my front legs. Then the world went black, as it had done once before, on the bipeds' battlefield. And, as it had done then, the darkness engulfed me.

As I began to drift in and out of consciousness, the dark periods became a welcome relief from the waking pain: a chelonian shell is sensitive, probably in the same way as the shell-covered areas on a biped's fingers and toes. To my intense relief, the damage had gone no further than my shell, which had done its job in protecting my insides. I always think it's very sensible that we chelonians wear our skeletons outside our bodies, rather than tucked away on the inside. The only other part of me which had suffered was a foreleg, where the edge of my shell must have been brought down hard as it cracked. The scaly skin of my leg was creased and cut, with a thick, uncomfortable crust where a trickle of blood had oozed out.

That was a strange, twilit summer for me. The sheep took no notice, probably viewing my inert and withdrawn body as just one more stone in their field. As soon as possible, though, I made my way lopsidedly down to the stream, where I could at least drink and get into the shelter of the shrubs growing there. Then my bodily systems slowed down again, almost to hibernation levels, so I didn't need much food; an occasional nibble at the nearest greenery was sufficient.

When autumn came, I sought deeper shelter; the shrubs would just have to do. Pushing my way in by using the undamaged side of my shell, I dug down painfully slowly, the leaves and debris falling back to help cover me. But the sounds of bipeds and their machines seemed to follow me, as I drifted uneasily into that year's hibernation.

A good winter's sleep helped to restore my equilibrium, though my leg was very stiff and the cracked part of my shell, despite forming scar tissue, would take much longer to become strong again. I emerged from hibernation very late, that year; the young birds were already fledging, and the watercress was abundant.

But when I finally felt whole again and ready to rejoin the world, I was in for yet another shock. The stream was no longer at the bottom of a sheep field; now it formed the boundary of a small, fenced garden. A low-level house loomed at the top of the slope, casting its shadow over close-mown, scentless turf which led down to an area still wild with turned earth, bushes – and me. I was trapped in a biped garden.

Actually, my situation was better than it first appeared, as long as the bipeds left that wild area alone, and didn't discover my presence in their domain. The house-owning bipeds must have been content with their scentless turf and their small flower beds, since they didn't seem at all interested in the wild area. I would occasionally glimpse them: a male and a female, elderly and walking slowly using sticks.

I was safe for the time being, even if my new domain was severely restricted. I had adequate food – mainly dandelions and watercress, supplemented by grass – and shelter. So I lived quietly for several years in my new smallholding, alongside my biped neighbours but unknown to them.

The first sign of change was when I heard biped voices, speaking quickly and stridently. These voices were quite unlike the gentle tones of the elderly bipeds, which had occasionally drifted down to me from their part of the garden on sunny afternoons – no doubt while they were enjoying their afternoon tea. But those elderly bipeds must have gone, perhaps just as the Major had gone, to leave a new set in charge. This time, though, I had little chance to wonder about their intentions.

The well-remembered sound of a digger reached me too late. It roared through the garden making straight for the wild area, and bore down on my basking place beside a bush. There was no time to escape, and no sanctuary within reach anyway. I could only scramble into the bush, and withdraw tightly into my shell.

As the roaring mechanical monster closed in on my shelter, the world suddenly seemed to turn upside down and then spin dizzily downwards, before a shock of flowing water hit my shell and I went tumbling downstream. Eventually, I came to rest against a clump of dense vegetation growing from the bank. Instinct gave me the strength to make one final effort to survive; I tried to climb out of the stream. But this bank was steep.

Chapter 12: The law of tort
Survival of the fittest

The chelonian fittest for those circumstances – half-submerged in a stream – would quite naturally be a turtle rather than a tortoise, but I was too busy to think about that, at the time. And as far as physical fitness is concerned, I've never considered myself as being amongst the fittest of creatures; we tortoises don't go in for biped-style weight-lifting or bending and stretching, or canine-style running, and we definitely prefer to leave swimming to our turtle cousins.

On this occasion, though, I had no choice but to use all my remaining strength in trying to get out of that water. The shock of falling out of the digger's scoop had been disorientating, despite the cushioning effect of my accompanying bush. My situation wasn't improved by cold water, either, or by the mini-waterfalls which had sent me tumbling downstream. But that clump of vegetation, firmly rooted to the bank, had given me something to cling to till the world stopped spinning and I found myself more or less right-side up. The stream was narrow at this point – little more than a hare's-leap across – but that didn't help me: each time I tried to climb out, the steep bank sent me slithering back down towards the water, and I knew that if I landed wrong-side up in the stream, I wouldn't be able to right myself. So each attempt at climbing out had to be slow and steady, but I could feel my strength beginning to fail as the cold and damp seeped into my shell. If I couldn't get out of that water very soon, my bodily systems would start the process of shutting down – permanently.

My whole instinct was now concentrated solely on survival. All senses were deteriorating as the cold blackness took hold, so that I was scarcely aware of help, when it came. Gentle hands closed around my shell and hoisted me clear; I seemed to be floating through air, till I came to rest on firm earth. Then blackness overcame me.

I roused, eventually, to any tortoise's best-loved sensation: the warmth of the sun permeating my shell. With my bodily systems functioning properly again, I spluttered as the water I'd swallowed came back up. I'd managed not to breathe it in, though, since we tortoises instinctively use the back of the tongue to stop water 'going down the wrong way', as the bipeds say, even with an open mouth: another of nature's very sensible precautions. As I spluttered, I heard a far-off biped voice, sounding concerned. Perhaps I was back with the Major...

Later, when my senses had returned more fully, I found myself on sunlit grass, with two juvenile male bipeds stretched out alongside me, stroking my shell and studying me carefully. It was that stroking of my shell which made me sense that I was in safe hands; the same hands which had hoisted me clear of the stream.

When I next woke, I was in a straw-lined box; clearly these bipeds knew something about tortoises, and meant me no harm. Actually, though, I began to doubt that, when my box was lifted into one of those cars which modern bipeds seem to love so much. Too weary to care where I was going, I settled down. The ride was much smoother than the horse-drawn cart in which I'd arrived at Treshillick all those years ago. But this time the journey was short, then my box was carried into a white room with lingering smells of various animals. A white-clad biped lifted me out onto a clean, dry surface. Competent hands explored the wound on my foreleg – which had broken open again during my attempts to climb out of the stream – and my damaged shell, which had suffered from the fall. A strange light was suddenly shone into my eyes, too. Then a pinprick made me feel drowsy again, and when I woke up, my injured leg hardly hurt at all; it had a white cloth wound around it to keep it steady. My shell had been properly cleaned, too. Then I must have travelled in my box again, drowsing, back to the bipeds' house by the stream.

A few days later I felt ready to explore my new surroundings. As a first step I stood vertically on tipclaws, biped-style, to peer over the side of the box. It turned out that the box wasn't very strong; my weight tipped it over very conveniently, so the side became the floor and I simply walked out, complete with my bandage, leaving a cascade of straw behind me. Now things became very interesting, as I was actually inside a biped house for the first time in my life. I made my way towards the light coming from a see-through wall, passing various objects which resembled unusually straight tree trunks. The garden was on the other side of the wall, so I set off to find the way out, searching for a gap in the see-through wall like the gap in the stone wall at Treshillick. But before I could find the gap, I found the bipeds, who seemed touchingly pleased to see me.

There were two adults – male and female – and the two juvenile males I'd already met in the garden. The adult male had been holding a book, larger than the ones the Major used to read to me. He happened to put it down very close to me, so I was able to peer at it long enough to realise that on the front was a picture of a tortoise. The book must have contained some useful information, because the biped family proceeded to offer me a selection of tasty titbits, some of which were reassuringly familiar – watercress and dandelions – while others were new to me. My favourite was a refreshingly crunchy yet juicy snack, which I later learned is called cucumber, and it's still one of my favourites now. My whole attention being so fixed on that first taste of cucumber, I scarcely noticed that I was accepting it directly from the hand of one of the juvenile bipeds – until I got a bit over-excited and my jaws closed not just on a piece of cucumber, but on a piece of biped finger, too. Its owner made a short, surprised sound, but didn't really seem to mind. Anyway, this was the first biped I'd ever allowed to feed me, other than Rosie, George and the Major. Perhaps things were going to turn out well after all.

While I was eating, the juveniles were studying some marks on my shell:

"Look, I can just make out this letter... and this one... d'you think it could be his name?"

"Let me see! I'm sure it is – someone's painted it on for him – I think maybe it used to say *Jerry*..."

A memory stirred, of my previous juvenile male bipeds, long ago in the meadow at Treshillick. George, and Rosie's brother Bob, with a tin of strong-smelling white fluid and a small brush, one sunny afternoon while I was dozing gently beside the old wall. A cool sensation – not unpleasant – on my shell, then George saying proudly:

"There, Bob, finished! Jerry's got his own 'dentification now, just like us, so he'm can't never get really lost."

Good for George! In our natural state, of course, we tortoises have no need of names, but I've noticed that the bipeds do like to name everything, and everyone. And anyway, I'd become so used to being called Jerry, all those years ago, that to keep the same name with my new family gave me a strange, comforting feeling of being connected to my past. George, Bob, and particularly my constant companion Rosie, would never be forgotten; nor would my first biped friend, the Major, who'd given me the name Jerry in the first place.

My new juveniles called out to their male parent, whom they addressed as Dad, just as George had done, and who was absorbed in his book, again:

"Look, Dad! We've found the remains of his name – it's Jerry! It suits him, don't you think?"

The adult male agreed enthusiastically:

"Wow! I've always wanted a tortoise, and Jerry's exactly the name I'd have chosen for him, myself."

So that was settled. Like one of the Major's books, I still had my name on the cover, with the essentials stored safely inside, plus all the information I've learned about bipeds and their ways, during all my travels. I think I must be what the bipeds call a mobile library.

Anyway, I recalled my attention to the present, and the cucumber. When I'd finished my meal, my new biped family courteously accompanied me to their garden. The adults had already started building an enclosure which would become my private pasture, with covered sleeping quarters and a low wall separating my part of the garden from the steep bank of the stream. This seemed to me a very good idea, after my recent experiences. Meanwhile, the juveniles were keen to show me around, pointing out every flower bed and every patch of clover or dandelions which they thought might interest me. It was a small garden, though naturally any enclosure seemed small compared to Treshillick. But this garden was perfectly adequate for my purposes, particularly as it came with the added benefit of sympathetic bipeds.

There was only one problem with these new arrangements: the bipeds didn't live here all the time. Gradually, as I became more familiar with my new family's speech patterns, I understood that their little house in Cornwall had belonged to an elderly relative (elderly in purely biped terms, of course), who'd died recently. So my new family travelled regularly from their own home, elsewhere in the south of England, to clear out the little house, tidy its garden, and sell it. All this sounded to me horribly like the sale of the Treshillick estate, until I learned that they were going to sell the house to bipeds who would actually want to live in it, rather than knock it down and build something else.

Personally, I'd have been happy to live in the Cornish garden by myself while my new bipeds were away, as a sort of caretaker, but they didn't seem to think that was a good idea. They were worried about my bad eyesight, coupled with my undoubted ability to find a way out of my enclosure and then perhaps go tumbling down the bank to end up in the stream again. This was because the white-clad biped who'd treated my leg – called the vet, probably because he's there to vet animals' health – had said that I can't see as clearly as I should, although I hadn't noticed that myself, being so used to it. Anyway, the vet wanted my biped family to take extra care of me, giving me lots of good things to eat and medicine to help my shell get stronger. That all sounded very sensible to me, but it meant my travelling to and from Cornwall with the bipeds, in their car.

In any case, summer was turning to autumn by now, so I ought to have been starting to prepare for hibernation. But my routine had been completely disrupted, and the vet wanted me to take food and medicine for a few weeks longer before letting my bodily systems slow down, so I ended up staying awake much later than usual, that year. I didn't mind travelling with the bipeds, who placed my box carefully in their car each time, but it was too late in the year for me to explore much of the garden at the biped family's own home. So that was when they built the Shell Garage for me and lined it with warm, dry straw. I would doze peacefully just outside it in the autumn sunshine, feeling safe and enjoying the tasty snacks which the bipeds brought me each day.

Once the weather became colder, the bipeds made me very comfortable inside their house. I had a straw-lined box beside the see-through wall – they called this the French windows, though I didn't see why the

English couldn't use their own windows – where I could feel close to the seasonal changes going on in the garden beyond.

So that brings me back to where I started this tale of my life amongst the bipeds, since that year's delayed hibernation is how I came to be inside a biped house on the day of the winter solstice. And that, in turn, is how I came to have my little accident with the fir tree which my biped family had placed indoors, just as I'd decided to take some exercise before winding down to my expected hibernation.

But the vet wasn't keen on the idea of my hibernating that year, what with all my recent excitements, plus my ongoing bandage, although of course I still had three good legs to rely on, whereas a biped in my situation would have to function as a uniped. Anyway, the vet wanted me to go for a consultation with a Reptile Specialist.

I was impressed – after all, it sounds very grand for me, a small tortoise, to have my own Specialist – and a few days later I had a thorough health check. My Specialist paid particular attention to my injured leg and my shell, which admittedly wasn't exactly looking its best, after all my adventures. Then he turned his attention to my eyes: he studied them, and shone lights into them, and moved my head gently from side to side. Eventually he decided that although my eyesight is very poor, he couldn't really do much to improve it. I was actually quite relieved – all that poking about with lights had been quite enough for me – and of course my Specialist must already have decided that the usual biped-style remedy would be tricky for me because, having no external ears, there'd be nowhere to park a pair of glasses. Perhaps I could have tried goggles, but I really don't think I'd like elastic round my head. I couldn't have contact lenses, either, because I blink from my bottom eyelids upwards, so I'd be forever pinging my lenses out all over the place.

I was perfectly content with the results of my consultation: although it would have been nice to be able to see better, we tortoises don't rely on eyesight as much as bipeds do. More importantly, my Specialist had told my new biped family about the best foods for me to eat, and how to help me prepare for next year's hibernation. He even gave them some extra strong medicine to help my battered shell. So I was relieved to go home with my bipeds, and spend my time alternately dozing and eating light snacks, safe in my box in their house.

The next spring saw me dividing my time between the little garden in Cornwall, and my biped family's own home in another part of southern England, called Hampshire. They didn't want to leave me behind in Hampshire, either, when they travelled to Cornwall, just in case I should overturn myself in the garden, or go falling into things like streams. I didn't mind the travelling, though, as any trip in the bipeds' car was far more comfortable than most of my previous journeys had been.

By midsummer, my family had found another set of bipeds who wanted to buy the little house in Cornwall. This caused great excitement, and great activity, as my family had to clear out all their own possessions. They also had to answer lots of questions about the house, writing their answers on lots of pieces of paper which looked something like a book. There were questions about the garden, too, and that's where I became involved.

The female of my biped family, who seemed to enjoy this sort of thing, was clearly amused when she brought the papers out into the garden one sunny afternoon, and flopped down on the grass beside me. By now, I could understand my biped family's speech patterns just as well as I used to understand the Major's, so I settled down to listen. There was one question which she particularly wanted to refer to me, although I missed quite a few of the most difficult-sounding words:

"Please confirm... there are no rights... to operate a ferry across the stream..."

Evidently delighted, she announced:

"Oh, Jerry! You're the only one who's travelled by stream, so they must mean *your* right to operate a ferry! After all, the rest of us could simply run down the bank and leap across. Your ferry, though: maybe you could operate it aboard a pond-yacht? Even then, the stream's so narrow that you'd meet yourself coming back! But you did tumble downstream, so let's call it Tortoise-shell Falls; I'll write a suitable reply..."

After a pause while she scribbled happily on another piece of paper, she read out her reply:

"We confirm the right to operate a ferry. For timetable and details of fares please go to www.jerrysferry@tortoise-shellfalls.com."

I didn't understand that last part, and anyway I wouldn't recommend embarking on that stream to anyone. But the female biped decided she'd better be careful, in case anyone believed there really was a ferry. Apparently, if I received income from it, my bipeds would be in trouble over the agreement to sell the house; as far as it related to the law of tort, that is.

So she tried out a different reply, which she called *Ode to a Tortoise*:

> There was a small tortoise called Jerry,
> Who thought he'd try running a ferry
> Across Tortoise-shell Falls,
> Where he took lots of calls:
> "Is the crossing quite lengthy?" "Not very."

I felt rather proud; quite apart from those Falls being named in my honour, no one had ever written any sort of ode to me before – not even when I lived in Greece. The female biped went on to tell me what she hoped the other bipeds' response might be:

> A tortoise-run ferry? The notion!
> That crossing would be in slow motion.
> And supposing it blew?
> There'd be need of a crew
> To dole out the sea-sickness potion.

But with or without the help of Greek odes, my new biped family finally sold the little house beside the stream in Cornwall, and I took up full-time residence with them in Hampshire, in a safe garden with a sturdy Shell Garage.

Chapter 13: Dogged footsteps
Tails of friendship

Domestic bipeds are generally fairly predictable, but I couldn't have predicted the apparent lapse of judgement when my bipeds suddenly brought home the newest member of our family: a dog! The idea of chelonians and canines sharing a garden would make any self-respecting tortoise shudder in its shell – if tortoises could shudder, that is – and at first I wasn't at all sure that my nerves would stand it, particularly as my early experience of the canine species hadn't been very encouraging.

It was during the bipeds' war when everyone was hungry, not just the bipeds themselves, and everyone felt threatened. The few dogs I saw in Morocco, and later in Greece, looked intimidating as they padded softly, their faces intent. But they tended to keep well away from us chelonians; in fact, they hardly seemed to notice our existence as they went in search of more appetizing prey. The same was true of the feline species, efficient hunters always ready to spring as they stalked rodents or birds, with muscles rippling and narrowed eyes glittering. Although these prowling carnivores always ignored me, instinct still warned me to keep well out of their range.

Then there were the farm dogs at Treshillick, though these were working dogs, who knew their place on the estate, and in any case they were always well-fed at the house itself. No one in the field ever felt threatened by them. Sometimes, when the Major came to see me, he would bring his own particular canine companion with him. But this was clearly no working dog; he was large, friendly and golden-coloured, and loved nothing better than to retrieve a stick or a ball which the Major would throw across the meadow for him. His name was Barkleigh, though this seemed to vary slightly, when he'd become so involved in his nose-down canine affairs, at the far side of the field, that he would ignore the Major's call. Then the Major would sound as if he were once more on a biped battlefield, as he shouted:

"Barkleigh! Heel, Sir!"

The dog would respond with a cheerful *woof!* as he bounded effortlessly across the grass. Skidding to a halt beside the Major, somehow he always managed to avoid trampling me with his great paws.

Barkleigh also had the distinction – as the Major mentioned more than once, with evident pride – of being the only canine at Treshillick to have won an official award: a bronze medal. Apparently, dogs and their bipeds have an association called the Kennel Club – rather like the Cornish Bards or the Girl Guides, I think – which gives awards in various categories (perhaps I misheard that last word; according to biped-style logic, it probably ought to have been dog-egories). So it seemed to me that the full name of the Major's evidently well-heeled dog must be Sir Barkleigh Woof, KCB (Kennel Club: Bronze).

Anyway, Barkleigh was always a cheery, modest individual who evidently had no intention of standing on ceremony, despite his status. Frankly, though, any dog who could produce as much slobber as Barkleigh did, would find it difficult to stand on ceremony in any event, however many awards he'd won.

The canine lifespan is naturally much shorter than the biped version, which must be due to all that mad dashing about, coupled with an unaccountable desire for endless walks and general canine over-excitement at the least provocation. In fact, I'd often hear the Major affectionately telling Barkleigh that he was barking mad. I really couldn't disagree with that view, although I did become very used to Barkleigh's occasional company in my field, where he enabled me to conduct my first field study of canine behaviour.

All this provided very useful experience when it came to my next canine encounter, which wasn't until many years later, in the garden of my bipeds' house in Hampshire. I'd already been living with my new family for some time, enjoying the peace of the garden which, until then, I'd shared only with the birds, occasional small mammals, and an assortment of insects. The different species all tended to keep a respectful distance from each other, although when I returned to the garden in spring, I would usually find that in my absence a mouse had taken up residence in my Shell Garage, having found it vacant. I've never minded giving a mouse houseroom, of course, except that it's rather startling when, still rather sleepy, you arrive home to snuggle down into the straw for a quiet doze, and someone else, suddenly fully awake, starts climbing over your shell, heading hurriedly in the opposite direction.

The only unwelcome residents of an English garden are generally the ants, who turned out to be plentiful in that part of Hampshire – something to do with the particular type of soil – and who are no respecters of anyone's privacy. In fact, hordes of ants taking a short-cut across the garden, via my shell, were always springtime's greatest irritation in my bipeds' garden. Then, in late summer, the ants would suddenly sprout over-sized wings and make themselves even more of a nuisance than usual, by lying around on everyone else's exteriors while trying to get used to the idea of flying. The garden's other inhabitants were always relieved when the ants finally got the hang of their wings and took off.

So that was the general situation in my bipeds' garden, until the arrival of the canine who unexpectedly became my friend. I first met Misty on the lawn, one warm afternoon in springtime. Tumbling about like an oversized ball of white fluff, she was little more than a puppy while I, of course, was already an experienced tortoise of the world. I learned from the bipeds that Misty's subspecies is called the West Highland terrier: I don't think hers has an alternative name to match mine, which was a relief at the time because, being officially called a Greek or spur-thigh tortoise myself, I couldn't imagine why anyone would want to be known as a West Highland or fluff-thigh dog.

At that first meeting in the garden, Misty seemed terrified of me; unusually terrified, from all I've learned about the general fearlessness of terriers since then, mainly from my observations of Misty herself. But she was introduced to me slowly and carefully by our biped family over the course of a few days, and I must admit that Misty was very courteous towards me right from the start. I think she felt an instinctive respect for my age and experience, despite my lack of physical stature.

Gradually, we became thoroughly used to each other, until we would spend sunny afternoons snoozing side by side on the lawn, as I already had the run (or perhaps more appropriately, the amble) of the whole garden in complete safety, since it was level, securely fenced, and had no stream. This was a relief when I first arrived in the garden, since I'd had quite enough of streams after the incident at Tortoiseshell Falls in Cornwall.

It seemed that my biped family had rescued Misty, too, though not from a stream: she was the last of her litter and, like me, in need of immediate help. I never knew the details of Misty's background, because that was a communication which, as an excitable juvenile, she either couldn't or wouldn't make, and by the time she was full-grown, she'd evidently forgotten everything except her life with our biped family. It strikes me that dogs are always intent on living purely in the present, rather than storing away a lifetime of experiences as I prefer to do, so that I can think them over at leisure. Perhaps that's because dogs need to live at a much faster pace than we chelonians do, in order to cram everything into their short lives, so they simply don't have time to chew things over in the same way.

Misty didn't chew food over in the same way, either, though she never hurled herself at her food in quite the same dramatic way as Barkleigh had done – or with quite such messy results. In fact, I think one reason Misty was so fond of my company was because I posed no threat to her at mealtimes, our diets being so completely different. She took no interest in mine, and I preferred not to think about hers. Whenever I was inside our bipeds' house, during spring and autumn, I was only too glad to steer well clear of the contents of Misty's food bowl, and she helped herself to mine (a piece of cucumber, actually), only on the one occasion, shortly after we first met. Unfortunately, the cucumber seemed to stick to her tongue, so she tried to prise off the now-sticky green mess with her sharpest and most pointed teeth – appropriately called canines, I believe – all of which caused some confusion and a lot of very unpleasant-looking drool. I think Barkleigh would have been proud of her, though I hadn't realised that a dog could contort its face into such an interesting variety of expressions in so short a time.

Misty was always very glad to welcome me back to the garden when I emerged from hibernation each spring: I think that, secretly, she missed my company during the winter. She could be something of a terrier-ist at times, though, mainly when she was playing with her favourite ball, which she used to roll towards me in the eternal hope that I might join in her game. I was forever trying to make her understand that even if I felt inclined to do so, I could only play extremely slowly (by her standards). But with the usual optimism of her kind, she invariably thought I was just letting her win at whatever game she'd decided we were playing. So Misty always considered me as the perfect gentleman, which made her very fond of me, as did the food situation – once she'd tasted my cucumber and learned to leave it alone, of course.

But Misty's favourite game always sent me ambling straight into the nearest cover. A seemingly all-weather game, it was invariably played during the early afternoon, and was eagerly anticipated by Misty anytime from midday onwards. Played with our female biped, who called the game muzzleball, its necessary equipment consisted of a medium-sized ball controlled (more or less) by Misty, and an ancient-looking wooden pole with a net at one end, called a lacrosse stick, wielded by our female biped. Having checked that I'd stowed myself safely away, the female biped would start the game – accompanied by high-pitched barking from Misty, already jumping up and down with excitement – by hurling the ball out of the net at the far end of the stick. As the ball landed on the grass it was immediately pounced on by Misty, who proceeded to charge at high speed across the lawn, pushing the ball with her muzzle and evidently intent on some goal of her own, usually in the middle of a flower bed.

Meanwhile, the female biped would come running up behind her, by now panting almost as much as Misty herself, and still wielding the lacrosse stick. This now proved its worth, not only for picking up the ball to throw it again without the risk of losing a chunk of biped hand to Misty's over-enthusiastic jaws, but also for plunging in front of the ball to stop it before it could do too much damage to the garden. This became particularly important if Misty happened to be hurtling along with the ball now apparently attached to her muzzle – *tail up, nose down,* seemed to be Misty's motto in all things – in the direction of a favourite shrub, or a delicately-stemmed flower, or even a delicately-shelled tortoise...

Apart from that brief bout of madness each day, Misty and I shared the garden very peaceably. She would flop down beside me while she recovered her breath after the latest game of muzzleball. Then we would spend the rest of a warm afternoon relaxing together under the cherry tree, each appreciating the sweet scents of the garden in our own way, and enjoying the sights and sounds as the bees and other insects went about their business, and the birds hopped across the lawn.

Mind you, we did have the occasional near-emergency, if I should happen to be sauntering through a flower bed just where Misty was busily digging a hole for a particularly special bone; having such poor eyesight, it would have been easy for me to tip myself straight in. I always realised in time, though, owing to the freshly-dug earth being tossed all over the place, and the noise of Misty's scraping paws and panting breath as she concentrated on her task. But it used to make me wonder, sometimes, whether Misty was planning our very own version of a story I remember Rosie reading to me, all those years ago at Treshillick: Winnie-the-Pooh and his newly-dug Heffalump Pit. If so, I didn't think the idea of my being the one to fall into the pit was particularly good. So I made sure I steered clear of Misty's excavations, as much as possible.

Generally speaking, though, we got along very well, and with Misty around, life in the garden was never dull. Apart from the companionship, I must admit that having my own guard dog could be a great comfort at times, such as on one of those rare occasions when I overturn myself. This can sometimes happen because, as spring turns to summer and the sun's rays become stronger, I too become stronger and enjoy some rather more active pursuits around the garden. In midsummer, when my shell has absorbed so much sunlight that I feel rampantly fully-charged, I like to patrol the perimeter of the entire garden at least once daily, at my full speed, which is no problem until I come to an obstacle. Then I find myself in the same situation as had arisen indoors, over the bipeds' midwinter fir tree: instinct tells me to keep going straight on, with the tenacity of my kind. As, of course, my famous ancestor did, in that well-documented race he had with the hare. And won. Except that I don't think he had to negotiate bipeds' garden obstacles such as garden rakes and ladders.

Not that I go about actually trying to climb ladders; but when faced with an obstacle, I carry on pushing a way doggedly (as it were) through whatever the obstacle happens to be, failing which I set about climbing over it. If the obstacle happens to be large and unyielding, or if I misjudge it or take it too fast (since my full speed can be satisfyingly fast), I might lose my balance and in that case, over I go. Once on my back, I can't then right myself, as my shell is too domed for me simply to be able to roll over again and shove my legs down. So I need help.

Enter a dog, barking. Misty provided me with my very own, reliable early-warning system in alerting our bipeds, as she would be seriously alarmed at finding me on my back with my legs flailing in the air, and my neck straining to prevent my head from

148

falling too far backwards. Any fellow-creature helpless and unable to right itself is an unnerving sight, so off she would dash, barking frantically, to find one of our bipeds who would come and set me to rights. Rather touchingly, Misty then liked to sniff gently at me to make sure I was unharmed: only then would she calm down, heave an enormous doggy sigh, and plump down in the grass beside me. All that excitement would then make us both doze off. This overturning only happened to me rarely, once or at most twice each summer, but whenever it did, in the sunny garden we shared for so many years, it always produced exactly the same degree of alarm in Misty, my personal guard dog, as it had done on the first occasion.

Our bipeds used to say it was little wonder that the garden as a whole wasn't exactly over-productive, contending as it did with the combined efforts of a mountaineering, gourmet tortoise and an excavating, ball-wielding dog. But on warm afternoons, my canine friend and I could usually be found sharing a patch of dappled sunlight together, relaxed and, in fact, quietly enjoying each other's company.

And that's how I'll remember Misty. Because, as anyone who's ever had a dog for a friend will know, that canine lifespan passes far too quickly, at least in comparison with the lifespan of a chelonian, or even a biped.

So, when Misty no longer wanted to play muzzleball, and didn't even try to roll her ball across the grass in my direction in quest of a friendly game, I knew something had changed inside her. I rather think she knew it, too, but she instinctively understood the inevitability of it all, and faced it with that tenacious canine courage of hers.

Our vet did his best for her. So did our biped family, who took her to a Canine Specialist, just as they had once taken me to a Reptile Specialist, long before Misty came on the scene. But, despite all that her own Specialist could to do for her, Misty gradually became less and less active until, on those last warm, balmy days at the very end of her life, one of our bipeds would carry her out to the garden, so that she could lie quietly beside me on the grass in the dappled shade of the cherry tree. She enjoyed that, and she still had enough strength to lift her head and sniff gently at me. I like to think that simply by my presence, there on the lawn beside her, I was able to bring my own share of comfort, with that deep understanding of life's natural cycle, which all of us in the animal kingdom possess by instinct.

Ours was an unlikely friendship: between a short-lived, exuberant dog and a long-lived, contemplative tortoise. But for all our differences of taste and behaviour, it was a real and trusting companionship enjoyed by two very different creatures, who just happened to share a biped family's garden for all those idyllic summers. It was a unique period in my life, with a companion I'll never forget.

Chapter 14: Salad days
A leaf out of Jerry's book

My years in the bipeds' garden in Hampshire were a settled and happy time, even though that particular period of my life didn't last as long as I might have expected, as things turned out. But despite being so generally peaceful, that time certainly had its own excitements as far as I was concerned, involving me in some very pleasant meanderings and even some slightly unusual excursions.

The earliest of these trips came shortly after I'd arrived in Hampshire, when I was taken on a tour of the area by my new biped family. This was because the adult male, in his continuing quest to learn more about the chelonian lifestyle, had decided that we should join the Hampshire Tortoise Association. This seemed to be a sort of chelonian Kennel Club, which made me think of Barkleigh and wonder whether I, too, was about to be given an award. Actually, until then I'd had no idea there were enough tortoises in Hampshire to form an Association; to me, it conjured up an image of us chelonians setting off on a slow colonization of the Isle of Wight, as a sort of extra Galapagos Island. This might well have suited Gilbert White, as he'd lived in Hampshire too, with his tortoise companion Harriet. And as she'd originally come from the Galapagos Islands, I think Gilbert White and Harriet might have been founder members of the Hampshire Tortoise Association.

Anyway, the Association's summer meeting turned out to be quite a sociable occasion. On taking stock of my surroundings when I emerged from my travelling-box, I found myself on a lawn along with the other chelonian members of the Association, each of us having our own private enclosure, separated by wire fencing. This meant that we could associate as far as we wanted to, which wasn't really very far, given that the mating season was over. But as the day was warm and sunny, and some tasty snacks had been thoughtfully placed in each enclosure, it was all very pleasant. Meanwhile, the biped members were listening to a talk about the latest ideas for helping us with hibernation, after which they enjoyed the inevitable afternoon tea on the lawn.

So we all – my two adult bipeds and I – travelled home feeling rather full. The female biped confessed that she hadn't really learned very much about hibernation, as she'd been too involved in happily speculating on the forthcoming tea. Apparently she'd hoped it might include some delicacies designed specifically for the Association, her suggested menu being: roulade of lettuce on a bed of cabbage stalks, followed by dandelion compote with a cucumber coulis, all washed down with a fine carrot – no, I think she said *claret* – but in any case she was mistaken. This was a shame, since I rather liked the idea of an association of bipeds and chelonians sharing a meal which would clearly have been both delicious and nutritious. Still, her appetite certainly hadn't been spoilt by disappointment, as she'd been tucking in to the more usual biped-style titbits with enthusiasm.

To compensate for the female biped's woeful lack of knowledge about the Three Rs – Relaxed Reptile Refrigeration, which is such an important aspect of modern chelonian life – I considered starting work on my own inevitably weighty tome to be called *Modern Hibernation Principles in Theory & Practice*, though I doubted whether I'd be able to get it finished in time for the following winter.

My general interest in weighty tomes probably stems from my classical education, which I mentioned when first telling you about my origins. It began with the instinctive knowledge inherited from our revered Greek patriarch Ptolemy Tortoise, which had been passed down from time immemorial, and culminated in my time at the University of Bangor, which had been about two hours. But it's surprising how much knowledge can be absorbed in a short time, and stored away for future use, in much the same way as absorbing and storing the sun's rays.

My opportunity to go to university arose purely thanks to my biped family. During the years I lived with them, the two juvenile males reached adulthood, and going to university seemed to be an acknowledged rite of passage. First, though, they each had to choose which university to go to, and that's where the whole family became involved, including myself. Visits were arranged to universities a long way from Hampshire, and when an overnight stop was needed, the bipeds didn't want to leave me alone in the garden, with all its inherent dangers, so I accompanied them.

The trip to Bangor was the most memorable, since this included a sample lecture on psychology. The female biped had offered to remain outside the venerable old building, and perhaps find a grassy area where I could refresh myself after being in my

153

travelling-box. Just as the family were discussing this, a distinguished-looking biped in cap and gown approached us, and peered into my box with the greatest interest. He introduced himself as the Vice-Chancellor, and very courteously wouldn't hear of my being excluded from his forthcoming lecture, but cordially issued his personal invitation for me to attend. He even accompanied us into the lecture theatre, where the female biped whispered to me that I was truly an honoured guest.

We settled ourselves amongst the rows of tiered seating, the female biped carefully placing my box on the floor at her feet. I couldn't hear much of the lecture from my position amongst a forest of biped legs, so I decided it might be better if I were to climb out of the box – my tipclaws trick of tipping it over sideways should work well enough, again – and set off for the front. Besides, I wanted to investigate the lecturer's podium, as it seemed to be the fount of all knowledge about biped psychology; a branch of the subject which I'd been studying for many years.

My box tipped over surprisingly easily, but unfortunately there wasn't much space in front of it before the floor fell away to the next level. So I tipped over too, landing amongst the legs of the bipeds in the row in front of us. It gave those bipeds a degree of surprise (if not actually a degree in psychology), particularly when my family started scrabbling about amongst their ankles, amid stifled giggles. By now I'd recovered my balance, and I was just getting into my stride – my levels of both interest and energy being high – when I was apprehended by the female of the family. She and I then went outside to calm down.

This was a shame, because she'd been hoping to get to the volunteering stage for the psychologists' new brain scanner, as she felt that I'd be just the candidate they needed, and I could probably have provided enough material for an entire thesis. Once we'd all recovered, my family decided they'd at least learned an interesting new formula:-

Tiered Seating + Stalled Tortoise

= Exponential Disaster

But for all its brevity, my time at university certainly wasn't wasted, and the female biped remained convinced that I must be the only tortoise to attain *any* degree of higher education; even if it was only a single lecture. In fact, she went so far as suggesting that my formal title should really be *Jerry the Greek Tortoise PhD (almost)*. I rather like the sound of that, even now: it seems to formalise my long study of the bipeds.

Another of our long-distance university trips was to a place called Aberystwyth which, although it didn't involve me in a sample lecture, did involve me in a sunny afternoon stroll along a broad, pleasant promenade beside the sea. The seafront bipeds were all very courteous in giving me enough room to walk along their promenade slowly and steadily in my usual straight line: in fact, they all seemed touchingly pleased to find a member of the chelonian order amongst them. My family agreed afterwards that the whole place had come to a standstill. Certainly the biped population showed a gratifying interest in me: a group of bearded adult males dressed in black left their noisy, smelly motorbikes to come and see me; other bipeds bi-pedalling their bicycles wobbled alarmingly; several juveniles fell off their boards-on-wheels while skating to a sudden halt; buckets and spades, babies and dogs, all were abandoned as the bipeds came to see me. My family joked about setting up my nationwide fan club on the spot, but I wouldn't have liked that: too much publicity for my taste.

Once the juveniles of the family had each completed their education and set off for pastures new, the garden assumed a pleasant tranquillity. I still missed my canine companion Misty, but the juvenile bipeds returned regularly, and they would always come straight to the garden to seek me out; except if it was winter, of course, though I'm sure that even then, they would peer into my high-tech fridge to make sure all was well.

Not all my trips involved travelling such long distances as Bangor and Aberystwyth had done, and not all of them were with my biped family. My solitary excursions were just as interesting as far as they went – which wasn't very far, on the whole. With their juveniles away so much, the adult bipeds were spending more time at home; it seemed they'd retired to their house and garden. This meant they had more opportunity for that favourite pastime of English bipeds: home improvements. I'd already achieved some success in my own home improvements, of course, notably by adapting the idea of the fissure in the fishpond. As I mentioned when discussing gardeners' questing time in my bipeds' garden, this had enabled me to arrange a successful irrigation system for the watering of my summer crops.

Anyway, one of the bipeds' first home improvements was to replace all the fences around the perimeter of the garden. This gave me the opportunity for some very interesting excursions around the immediate neighbourhood, since the bipeds needed to remove each section of the old fence in turn, and replace it with wire netting while they prepared to install the new, stronger fence. But I was ready for them: waiting under cover in a nearby bush, I simply strolled over the newly-disturbed ground and dug down deep enough, hibernation-style, to push my way underneath the wire and into the next garden.

Each set of bipeds likes to organise their garden differently, naturally enough, so I was able to enjoy sampling some different plants – a sort of taster menu – as the next-door garden turned out to contain a wide variety of extremely tasty salad crops. By the time my own bipeds had realised I was missing and arrived, looking flushed, in their neighbours' vegetable plot, I'd tested each different crop for quality, and was perfectly satisfied with the results of my investigations. In fact, I was stretched out on top of a well-formed lettuce, still taking an occasional nibble while basking in the sun and feeling rather full.

Next, the bipeds tried putting bricks on the ground while preparing each new section of the fence. Fortunately, though, I was able to rely on my experience of clambering amongst the low walls of ruined temples back in Greece, so a few bricks presented no major obstacle to me. On the other side of this particular low wall was an unforeseen grassy slope, which sent me slithering, but I stayed right-side up and set off to explore our other neighbours' garden. This turned out to be unexpectedly dangerous: the bank which had sent me slithering ended in a pair of long metal lines, forming a track which had evidently been made by the bipeds for some particular purpose. I set off curiously along the track, past some miniature bushes and toy sheep on the grassy bank. Even more curiously, I came to an upright pole with a red-and-white striped arm sticking straight out. At that moment there was a sudden hissing sound, as a small-scale mechanical monster hurtled out of a dark hole in the ground and round a bend towards me, spewing steam. I headed for the bank – at least it would be easier to climb than the bank of the stream in Cornwall – just as the monster's many wheels let out a loud screeching sound, and it came to a shuddering halt on the track. By now thoroughly alarmed, I was climbing up the bank, scattering toy sheep in all directions, when once again biped hands closed around my shell and hoisted me clear.

These hands were small: they belonged to a juvenile biped who was evidently as startled as I was. Mixed with the shouts of the unknown juveniles, I heard my own adult bipeds calling, as they came running up:

"Oh, *Jerry!* You very nearly got run over!"

"Trust you to stray into the path of an oncoming, fully-functioning steam train!"

Then, from the small juveniles:

"Wow, it's lucky we'd set that signal to *Danger!*"

"Would your tortoise like a ride? He wouldn't fit inside a carriage – though I suppose we could try, if we take the roof off and he sticks his head and front legs out?"

"No, he'd probably tip the whole carriage over. But we could rig up a low-loader and give him a ride to the end of the line. It winds all the way round the garden, the station's right over there beside the pond…"

My own bipeds hurriedly declined all offers of giving me a ride on a steam train. I was quite relieved, as I'd had enough of miniature railways by then, and I was actually rather glad to be taken home by my bipeds. But for several days afterwards, they kept talking about a set of books they'd read to their own juveniles, years earlier, all about steam trains with names like Thomas the Tank Engine. They seemed to think I should feature in one of those books – as Jerry the Slow Engine.

Sometimes the visiting arrangements were reversed, and other bipeds came on excursions to see me in the garden, such as when my own bipeds went away on holidays which would be unsuitable for me. This was always the case when they were going to fly to another country: I didn't like that idea at all, as it brought pictures to my mind of those flying monsters of the genus *Spitfire*, during the bipeds' war. Now, though, on these occasions our neighbouring bipeds would come into the garden every morning and evening to give me some titbits, make sure I hadn't got too carried away with my excavations or overturned myself, and see me safely stowed away for the night. They seemed delighted that I'd usually found my own way to the Shell Garage and settled myself down amongst the straw.

159

If it happened to be spring or autumn, the neighbours also helped me to my indoor *vivarium* each evening, and outside again each morning, as the Shell Garage wasn't heated. If they arrived rather late in the morning, the neighbours would find me expressing my disapproval by a little huffing and puffing, and scrabbling at the edges of my *vivarium*. This was enough to make them realise that, with the sun already well risen, instinct had made me eager to be outdoors in my natural environment. Courteously, they then decided to get up a bit earlier each day, rather than keep me waiting! They seemed most impressed at the strength of my legs, too, as I propelled them, doggy-paddle style, encouraging whoever was carrying me towards the great outdoors to go a bit faster. Their evenings seemed to have been geared to ensuring that they could find me well before dark, and in good time in case I should be getting cold. For my part, I always made sure I didn't get lost or overturn myself: I'd never deliberately worry our kind neighbours, as they always showed such touching concern for me.

Another neighbour invited me on an excursion which sounded vaguely familiar: I was booked to make a guest appearance at a meeting of the Brownies, who turned out to be miniature Girl Guides. This neighbour was keen to come in every day to bring my lunch, while my own bipeds were away on one of their holidays; I think she really wanted to see me about my forthcoming visit to her Brownies, but I was more concerned with lunch, as it's always been my favourite meal. Anyway, the day of my visit arrived, and my own bipeds accompanied me to a very pleasant field where the Brownies were assembled. Amid much stroking of my shell, these juvenile females learned about the chelonian lifestyle, while I accepted the tasty titbits they offered. It was warm in the sunny field, so I actually dozed off before the end of my bipeds' lecture: this was unfortunate, as apparently the Brownies generally prefer their guests to be awake.

Meanwhile, my own bipeds continued with their home improvements. Apart from that memorable spring when the new windows and doors had been fitted to their house, the most notable of these was when they decided to make their house bigger by extending it into the back garden. I'd only recently woken from hibernation, and I was a little surprised by all the unaccustomed noise and activity as a succession of very dusty bipeds traipsed through the house and even climbed over my *vivarium*. So I insisted on going out in the garden regardless of the weather, to make sure that the bipeds' diggings didn't get too near to my pastures, or even to the Shell Garage itself.

The fissure in the fishpond caused problems, too: I didn't mind the bipeds' decision to have it fixed, because by then my own irrigation system was well-established, but mending the pond involved the arrival of a digging machine. That made me nervous, bringing back memories of Treshillick, particularly when the machine started mudslides dangerously close to some of my best crops.

So I continued to wonder, sometimes, whether it was entirely safe to leave my bipeds in charge of the garden each winter, while I was asleep. But all these events were merely diversions in the peaceful rhythm of my life with my retiring bipeds, which we all expected to continue for many years.

Chapter 15: Shell-tered accommodation
The retiring tortoise

I like to consider myself as something of a philosopher, what with my inheritance from Ptolemy Tortoise and my own experiences of living amongst the bipeds, but I've discovered that not all the bipeds' famous philosophers lived in ancient Greece. They have modern versions too, all over the world. A member of the modern variety seems to have been one of those Beatles whom I narrowly missed meeting in Cornwall, when they were too busy to attend the music festival at Treshillick. According to the female of my biped family in Hampshire, this particular Beatle suggested that 'life is what happens while you're busy making other plans', and this turned out to be true for the whole family – including myself.

At first, our joint retirement seemed promising, as the two adult bipeds and I settled into a comfortable routine in the well-established chelonian colony of Hampshire. We shared the garden very happily during the summer – despite our occasional differences of opinion over such matters as fences, vegetable plots and irrigation systems – and shared at least a part of the house itself, purely for my own personal fridge in winter, and for my *vivarium* in spring and autumn.

Within this perfectly satisfactory arrangement, we each continued to pursue our own individual interests. I renewed my acquaintance with the garden each spring, and then went on to inspect my burgeoning crops, checking their quality regularly and keeping a weather eye on their irrigation levels as summer progressed, before turning my attention towards hibernation each autumn. Meanwhile, the bipeds established various new interests in their newly-acquired state of retirement, some of which took them away from home rather more often than my own pursuits did.

One of these interests was the male biped's renewed passion for motorbikes. Apparently he'd owned a succession of these rather noisy and smelly machines in his youth, although he'd never gone in for the black outfit or the hairy face. Now, in his retirement, he'd acquired another of these machines, which turned out to be far less noisy and smelly than the ones we'd all encountered on the seafront at Aberystwyth. This motorbike lived beneath a sheltering roof, rather like my Shell Garage but alongside the house itself, with gates at the front so he could take it out onto the road, and open at the back so he could bring it into a gravelled section of the garden where he could work on it. Here, the adult male could often be found on sunny afternoons, rummaging in a box of tools and tinkering happily with his motorbike. The female of the family used to say that she was glad of the screening hedge, between the gravelled section where it stood and the rest of the garden, which meant she didn't have to look out at the motorbike's oily innards.

Whenever he had the opportunity, the male biped liked nothing more than to put on his special set of motorbike clothes, all topped off by a bowl-shaped helmet completely enclosing his head, which looked dark and forbidding but had a window at the front for his face. This was probably much the same as the goldfish bowls worn by the astronauts who accompanied their astro-torts, when they got their marching orders to try a joint migration of species into space. Anyway, the adult male of my biped family would set off to enjoy riding his motorbike around the open country roads of Hampshire. He always came home looking relaxed and very pleased with himself.

Except for the final occasion, when he didn't come home at all.

I was unaware of this at the time it happened, since he'd already helped me into my fridge for my long winter's nap. Although this turned out to have been my final contact with the adult male of the family, I'd had no sense of foreboding, as I'd had back at Treshillick when I'd seen the Major leave home in that large white vehicle with the red symbol on its side. This time, I'd already settled down in my straw-lined box, and was peacefully asleep beneath my Cornish tea-towel, having left the bipeds to enjoy their winter festivities.

So it was only on rousing, the following springtime, that I realised something was terribly wrong. Still drowsy, I was dimly aware of the usual household noises, but also of something distinctly *un*usual: the atmosphere in the house was permeated by a sense of unfathomable loss.

Hastened by a growing feeling of unease, my routine of gradual waking continued, as willing biped hands helped me to my *vivarium* with its heat and sun lamps. Those hands belonged to the female of the family, and they shook slightly as they picked me up. Then I heard a noise which seemed to come from somewhere deep inside her, and as she placed me gently inside my *vivarium*, I felt the slow splash of moisture from her eyes as it dropped onto my shell. It was all just the same as when Rosie had said goodbye to me on leaving Treshillick at the end of the bipeds' war. But as yet, I could make nothing of this sadness enveloping my newer female biped friend: she whispered something to me, but I was still too sleepy to make out what she was saying.

Once I'd roused into full consciousness, I realised that both the juvenile males of the family had come home; they, too, were evidently immersed in the pervading sense of desolation. But there was no indication that the adult male of the family was present. That sense of desolation, I now realised, was ominously similar to the feeling I'd experienced on surfacing into the Cornish springtime with the conviction that I would never see my friend the Major again. It was becoming obvious that once again, I was facing the loss of a biped friend. It was from the younger of the juvenile males that I finally learned what had happened, as he sat with me on his lap, under the cherry tree's spring blossom.

It had been during the bipeds' festive season, and the adult male – always affectionately referred to as *Dad*, but now in tones of agonised grief – had set off on his motorbike to visit an elderly relative who lived on the other side of Hampshire. His motorbike had been hit by a car, which was being driven very fast by a young male who'd drunk too much.

At first, I couldn't understand why drinking too much should make a biped drive a car too fast since, like most species, bipeds need to keep themselves well hydrated in order to stay alive and to function properly. But then I remembered the music festivals at Treshillick, and how angry the Major was when a few of the biped visitors cheerfully drank too much of a particular type of drink – alcohol – which eventually made them lose control of their mental and physical faculties. They would stagger about, shouting, and eventually fall over. I remembered wondering at the time why any creature would deliberately inflict that on itself, but alcohol seems to be another of those mysteries peculiar to the biped species.

Certain bipeds like to drink too much alcohol at their midwinter festive season, too, and that's what had caused the young driver to lose control of his car, in the case of my family. The biped phenomenon of tears isn't confined to the female of the species, and the drops were falling faster as the younger male of our family told me that Dad's helmet and protective clothing couldn't save him: he had died immediately.

Years earlier, by the time I'd realised that the Major had died, there were no bipeds left at Treshillick to mourn him. Now, for the first time, I was witnessing a biped family's grief for one of its own members. Winter had become spring by the time I emerged from hibernation and learned what had happened, but the family's grief was still palpable: that intense and prolonged grief to which bipeds generally are subject. The two juveniles – not actually juveniles any longer, but fully-grown adults, already scarred by their proximity to death – came home to be with their mother as often as possible. In between their visits, I kept her company as best I could, in our quiet and sadly reduced household.

She was determined to carry on alone, maintaining the large house and garden which had been the family home for so long. Meanwhile, my eyesight was fading more quickly now, so I appreciated a little more biped help with feeding, each day. It was during these quiet times – revered by the bipeds as breakfast, lunch and afternoon tea – when, sitting beside me on the lawn, my female biped friend would confide to me her own feelings of grief and loss. Gradually, though, overwhelming anger began to consume her other feelings, like a fire raging somewhere deep inside her and directed against the young driver who had caused the family's devastation. At these moments, her voice became choked and harsh, hot tears would fall, and she would cut up my salad and fruit with ferocious intensity. Suddenly she would realise what she was doing, and check herself, then hold me to her as she poured out her grief and pain.

Apparently she was to attend a special gathering – a Court – which sounded to me rather like a meeting of the Cornish Bards but far more serious. The Court would eventually decide what was to happen to the young driver: he would inevitably be kept confined in a special, secure place, living separately from the mainstream bipeds, probably for some years. After all, bipeds do have certain standards: apart from the times when they decide to kill each other in huge quantities during their wars, they're simply not allowed to go around killing each other at random. But my female biped, in her fury, told me she'd like to kill this particular specimen of the species herself:

except that bipeds aren't allowed to kill for revenge, either.

So she had to work through her loss and anger as best she could. Throughout that summer, she cared for me exactly as the whole family had always done, spending as much time with me as possible. But it was becoming apparent that her day-to-day living arrangements would need to change, and soon, to match her changed circumstances. At the onset of winter she settled me into my *hibernaculum* in my fridge, after weighing me just as her mate had always done. But despite all her care, it was with a slight sense of unease that I drifted into that winter's sleep.

I roused in springtime to find that she'd been doing a great deal of decision-making during the winter. The house and garden were too big for her to manage alone, and she'd started to look for somewhere smaller to live. Meanwhile, her two juveniles had also been busy: the elder already lived and worked in the north of England, while the younger had moved to Europe (I hoped he'd had a more comfortable journey than I'd had, coming in this direction all those years ago, in a biped troop-ship). The female of the family would need to be free to visit her offspring whenever possible, and also just to be away from home during the daytime more frequently than when she and her mate had retired and centred their attention on their home. All this would inevitably affect me, too, as my failing eyesight meant that I needed increasing daily help with feeding. So we would have to part: once again, I found myself needing a new home.

Over and over again, she told me how sorry she was, but she was determined to find me an even better home:

"You don't need to live in this sad atmosphere, Jerry – you deserve a better retirement than that. I can't go back to Cornwall myself – it would be too painful for me, we were all so happy there, as a family. But there's no reason why you shouldn't go back, is there: would you like that?"

I nudged her hand, to show her that I understood her completely, and once more I felt the splash of tears on my shell.

The female biped in charge of the Hampshire Tortoise Association was due to take her summer holiday in Cornwall that year, where she was to visit the bipeds in charge of the Cornwall Tortoise Association. So she offered to take me with her, which struck my remaining biped family and me as a very sensible idea. Before I left, though, the female biped of my family proudly announced that, on my behalf, she'd accepted honorary lifelong membership of the Hampshire Tortoise Association. Sitting with me under the cherry tree, she told me she'd secretly been hoping they'd offer me the Presidency. After all, as she pointed out, I'd already gained plenty of highly relevant experience by (almost) taking the podium in that lecture hall at Bangor, so why not in a town hall at Southampton? But it was probably all for the best: after the effort of actually getting to the podium, I'd probably just have fallen asleep, which wouldn't have made for an especially fascinating start to the members' meeting.

As we parted, the female of my Hampshire family bestowed on me that gesture of affection and friendship which the bipeds often demonstrate to each other, and sometimes to their canine companions, too. But I had never known such a gesture made to a chelonian, until she bent over me and, through her tears, placed on the top of my head the whisper of a kiss. In reply I nudged her hand, silently wishing her well and, eventually, happy.

So I set off once more for pastures new, in my travelling-box carefully placed inside a car. On my arriving in Cornwall, the local Tortoise Association bipeds courteously showed me around a large room in their house, the official headquarters of the Cornwall Tortoise Association, which was devoted entirely to a huge *vivarium*. This was divided into sections for several tortoises, and also had special covered and heated areas for eggs and hatchlings.

I spent the next few days enjoying a variety of tasty snacks in a private enclosure in their garden. To be honest, the enclosure was disappointingly small, given the overall size of the garden, but these bipeds did have a lot of tortoises to accommodate individually. Anyway, they evidently knew about the chelonian lifestyle, so I felt confident that they'd find me an appropriate new pasture.

On a warm, sunny afternoon, I was taken to meet the biped who wanted to offer me a home. This was an elderly female who, after a lifetime's career as a nurse in London, had retired to Cornwall with her mate. Now living alone after his death, she'd contacted the Cornwall Tortoise Association: she'd had a tortoise friend many years ago, and always wanted a chelonian companion of her own. She lived in a traditional Cornish cottage with an enclosed and well-stocked garden, which smelt good as I approached.

It was her voice I recognized first, and then the light in her eyes, lively and bright enough to penetrate my own. As she stroked my shell, her hands felt wrinkled, and almost as dry to the touch as my own limbs. But of course we're both older now, Rosie and I, in our respective processes of ageing. Still stroking my shell, she mused softly to herself:

"I wonder... Is it possible... That ragged scar on your shell: it wasn't there before, but maybe something dreadful happened to you, when Treshillick was bulldozed... It must have been touch and go, but you were always a survivor..."

Then, more confidently:

"And you're just the right size, too, as nearly as I can remember. Oh, it's all so long ago! Anyway, I'm so glad you're here with me now, we'll be company for each other, and of course I *must* call you by the old name, just in case..."

Suddenly she held me closer, peering intently at me:

"Wait a moment, though: what are those white marks on your shell – paint? I remember George, concerned with identification... Where are my glasses? Got them! Now, let's have a proper look..."

At this point, I thought it would be wise to give her one of my gentle nudges, just as I used to do in the meadow at Treshillick. That seemed to work:

"Oh, *Jerry!*"

Naturally, instinct tells me that Rosie cannot possibly live as long as I can: there will come a time when she and I must inevitably part. But she has younger family members, who visit her here in Cornwall where she and I both found refuge so long ago. And we've always understood each other perfectly: after all, Rosie and I are as good as family, with a history of shared experiences. I know I'm safe in her hands, as I was when she was a small evacuee in a strange place, and then a Girl Guide growing towards adulthood and increasingly confident of her own place in the world.

And so I've come full circle – another of those classical concepts expounded by Ptolemy Tortoise – back to Cornwall where my journeys around Great Britain began. I've been lucky enough to make good friends amongst the bipeds, and even with the occasional canine, along the way: the Major with his Barkleigh; George wielding his paintbrush, and Bob the London evacuee; my Hampshire family with their Misty; I even felt some affinity for the gentle, elderly biped couple who never knew that I was sharing their small piece of the old Treshillick estate; and my special companion Rosie.

Of course, I don't keep count of the passing years: I live by the ancient, unchanging rhythms of the earth. Happy simply to enjoy life's pleasures in my own quiet way, with the added benefit of a biped friend whose company I relish each spring and summer, in this mild Cornish climate. Then shafts of gentle autumn sunshine on my shell, and a last few tasty snacks while I linger outside the slate-roofed Cornish version of my Shell Garage, with its very own shingled forecourt and fragrant coastal garden. And then a safe hibernation to look forward to, renewing my strength for whatever next year may bring.

29639121R00101

Printed in Poland
by Amazon Fulfillment
Poland Sp. z o.o., Wrocław